AMERICA IN DECLINE

A CENTURY OF LEFTISTS DAMAGING AMERICA

DENNIS B. MALPASS

ISBN: 1484045165
ISBN 13: 9781484045169

DEDICATION

*For my grandchildren (the "grandies"): Dylan, Sydney,
Peyton, Keaton, Noah, Rylie, Bryce and Ethan:*

*May you live a long life
Full of gladness and health,
With a pocket full of gold
As the least of your wealth.
May the dreams you hold dearest,
Be those which come true,
The kindness you spread,
Keep returning to you.*

Irish proverb

TABLE OF CONTENTS

PREFACE

THIS BOOK IS A RESULT *of the overwhelming disappointment I felt when the American people re-elected the extreme leftist Barack Obama in 2012. I wanted to understand how a president could be re-elected in view of:*

- ▸ *a moribund economy,*
- ▸ *excessive unemployment and underemployment,*
- ▸ *incompetent foreign and domestic policies,*
- ▸ *irresponsible spending that has run the national debt to nearly $17 trillion, and*
- ▸ *abuse of presidential powers not seen since the administration of Franklin Roosevelt.*

As I searched for explanations, I gradually came to the realization that Mr. Obama's re-election was simply a recent manifestation of the country's ongoing slide to the left. Though it began incrementally long ago, it has undermined the American system of governance and inhibited free market capitalism. Personal liberties have been eroded. America is being transformed into a socialistic Nanny State, similar to many European countries in the early part of the 21st century. Furthermore, demographics and voting patterns make it a near certainty that America's slide leftward will continue well into the future.

This book incorporates personal perspectives accumulated over my 70+ years. It allowed me to vent about some pet peeves and, in a few places, permitted me to take a stroll down memory lane. I've dedicated the book to my grandchildren. Indeed, with apologies to the erudite reader, I've included background information such that, when my grandchildren become young adults and read the book, they should readily grasp historical contexts. Unfortunately, it is they and their descendants who will bear the full consequences of a leftist America.

I have been a life-long student of history. I've included excerpts from my readings on history and politics that I believe support assertions about what has happened to America and the direction in which the country is headed. This book is my view of what was, what is, and what is yet to come in America. My conclusions do not bode well for conservatives or the Republican Party.

If you are conservative, you will probably concur with many of the positions I have taken in this book. If you are an independent, I hope you will be open-minded and give serious thought to my contentions. Perhaps you will even come to agree with me on some of my assessments. However, if you are liberal, I recommend that you stop here. This book was not written for you; rather it's about you and your comrades. A principal point of this book is that leftists are largely responsible for America's ongoing disintegration into a socialistic Orwellian state. It is my belief that liberals have been harming this country for more than a century.

The opinions in this book are unadorned, sometimes bluntly stated and occasionally politically incorrect, but they are my own unvarnished viewpoints acquired over a lifetime of studying history and observing politics. They are opinions, not of a sophisticated Washington insider, but of an ordinary American citizen whose views were shaped in no small way by work experiences that began as a 13-year old boy delivering Times Picayune newspapers at 5 am in Biloxi, Mississippi, continued through many years as an industrial chemist in Texas, and concluded as a manager in Singapore. Mostly as part of my job, I was privileged to travel to four continents and dozens of foreign countries. I also had *occasion to visit more than 40 of the 50 states. I met many amazing, wonderful people all over America and the world. I've seen places and things that I could never have imagined as a youngster growing up in Biloxi all those years ago. But one of the most important lessons I learned was that America, despite her flaws, is the greatest country in the history of the planet. Jingoistic? Perhaps, but you must forgive me, for I was born in a simpler time, when pride in America was not politically incorrect.*

Has America made mistakes and done things that were less than honorable? Yes, of course, and we are incessantly reminded of America's historic flaws by a cadre of leftists. The cadre is comprised of activists with a variety of liberal agendas, including many from the following groups:

- ▸ *the Democrat Party,*
- ▸ *the mainstream media,*
- ▸ *ideological environmentalists,*
- ▸ *academia, and*
- ▸ *the entertainment industry.*

But, on balance, America has been a beacon of freedom to the world for more than 2 centuries. In large measure, that was due to its liberties, its free market capitalism and its extraordinary, hard-working, entrepreneurial citizens. America has been that "shining city on a hill" as President Ronald Reagan called it in his farewell address.

Nevertheless, over my three score and ten years, I've seen changes that are harbingers of the decline of that "shining city on a hill." Though some changes have unquestionably been positive, others have been quite harmful. In many instances, these changes have been wrought by leftist policies that began innocuously over a century ago. Little-by-little these have chipped away at the very foundations of America. The hatred harbored by some on the left today has divided and polarized the country to the point where the chasm between right and left may be impossible to bridge. Contrary to what President Reagan, the eternal optimist, believed in the 1980s, it appears to me that America's ongoing slide to the left means that our best days are behind us.

However, life goes on. Though a Reaganesque government in America may become a distant memory by the end of the 21st century, conservatives must persevere. There are a few measures that may postpone the inevitable (mentioned in Chapter 10). America may be diminished, but conservatives must continue the fight. Liberalism hasn't defeated conservatism. It remains true that conservatism wins most arguments based on reason and ideas, but conservatives have simply been out-worked, out-immigrated and out-maneuvered legislatively and politically.

Dennis B. Malpass
March 21, 2013
Magnolia, TX

ACKNOWLEDGEMENTS

THIS BOOK PROVIDED AN OPPORTUNITY *for me to speak from beyond to my progeny about America. It afforded a chance to explain my view on some of the things that went wrong and how the inevitable may be postponed. I must acknowledge friends, associates and family for their help on this book:*

Holly Malpass Balius
Elliot I. Band
Dina Malpass Graves
Joseph J. Ligi
Darrin V. Malpass
Sheila Phippeny Malpass
John Milam
Martin Scrivener
Debbie Malpass Shepard

During the early part of 2013, I inundated them with chapter drafts and questions about software, syntax and content. I thank them for their forbearance in reviewing the text and providing comments and suggestions.

These people provided helpful suggestions for which I am grateful. However, they do not necessarily agree with the premise of this book, nor do they necessarily share political opinions expressed by the author.

List of Abbreviations and Acronyms

ADHD	attention deficit hyperactivity disorder
ANWR	Arctic National Wildlife Reserve
CCD	climate change denier
CCS	carbon capture and sequestration
CFCs	chlorofluorocarbons
CIA	Central Intelligence Agency
CPUSA	Communist Party of the USA
DDT	From common chemical name: dichlorodiphenyltrichloroethane
DOD	Department of Defense
DOJ	Department of Justice
EPA	Environmental Protection Agency
FCCC	See UNFCCC
FDR	Franklin D. Roosevelt
GCM	general circulation models
GM	General Motors
GOP	Grand Old Party (another name for the Republican Party)
GWA	global warming alarmists
ICE	internal combustion engines
IPCC	Intergovernmental Panel on Climate Change (formed by the UN)

IQ	intelligence quotient
IRS	Internal Revenue Service (aka "Infernal Revenue Service")
JFK	John F. Kennedy
KGB	Russian secret service, counterpart to America's CIA; abbreviated from unpronounceable Russian words
LBJ	Lyndon B. Johnson
LED	light emitting diodes
MW	megawatt
NAACP	National Association for the Advancement of Colored People
NARAL	National Association for the Repeal of Abortion Laws
NASCAR	National Association of Stock Car Auto Racing
NGOs	nongovernmental organizations
NOW	National Organization of Women
OSHA	Occupational Safety and Health Administration
PEL	permissible exposure limit
PETA	People for the Ethical Treatment of Animals
ppm	parts per million
PTSD	post traumatic stress disorder
RINO	Republican in name only
SPCA	Society for the Prevention of Cruelty to Animals
UN	United Nations

UNFPA   United Nations Fund for Population Activities

UNFCCC   United Nations Framework Convention on Climate
             Change

USSR   Union of Soviet Socialist Republics

List of Tables

Chapter 1

CHANGE, LIBERALS AND THE MAINSTREAM MEDIA

Nothing in the world is permanent, and we're foolish when we ask anything to last, but surely we're still more foolish not to take delight in it while we have it. If change is of the essence of existence one would have thought it only sensible to make it the premise of our philosophy.

W. Somerset Maugham

That Was Then, This Is Now

AS THE MAUGHAM QUOTE ABOVE suggests, change is a fundamental part of the human experience and the natural world. Though it often comes slowly, it is relentless and inevitable. Change can be positive, but it can also be negative. If you are dissatisfied with changes in your life, you have little recourse. It cannot be magically undone. On the golf course, players are sometimes allowed a do-over called a "Mulligan" (named after an Irishman who wanted to hit another bad shot). However, life doesn't permit Mulligans. You must live with the consequences of your actions. You must accept the changes in your life, adapt to the new reality and move on. Better luck next time (or in the next election). Change for change's sake is not necessarily a good thing. This book is about change-- changes that started long ago but have put the United States of America* on a path of decline. This book is a direct result of my attempt to understand why America re-elected Barack Obama with his promises of hope and change.

I grew up in the 1950s. It was a simpler time—personal computers, cell phones, the Internet, and iPods were science fiction then. We played vinyl records ("45s") using Victrolas. Most of us did not have air-conditioning. Elvis, Sam Cooke, Buddy Holly and Chuck Berry were making their marks in popular music. Cars with fins and "wrap around windshields" were big. Few Americans had heard of Vietnam. The tumultuous 1960s were just around the corner. Unfortunately, it was also a time of appalling discrimination against African-Americans (and not just in the South). Though America continues to struggle with race, racial discrimination is not the overwhelming problem it once was. Who could have imagined during those racially troubled times that Americans would elect an African-American as President in 2008?

---

* In this book, I will often use America as shorthand for The United States of America. For political correctness (a subject of Chapter 8), I should apologize to our fellow North Americans (Canadians, Mexicans, Costa Ricans, etc.) and our friends in South America.

(Though it would have been much better for the country had it been Herman Cain.) Nevertheless, charlatans such as Al Sharpton and Jesse Jackson continue to foment racial strife. My chagrin about the election of President Obama was not because of the color of his skin, but because of the content of his character: he is a devout socialist. Yes, America must continue to fight all forms of discrimination. However, there are other issues that are far more troubling. Schisms between left and right, rich and poor, "haves" and "have nots" are threatening the very foundations of the country.

I have now graduated into the club comprised of what, when I was a young guy, we used to call "old farts." This book is an expression of the concern this old fart has about the future of America. The self-reliant country that my parents and grandparents knew no longer exists. I worry about the America my grandchildren and great grandchildren will inherit. Even during the span of my lifetime, profound changes have occurred---some for the better, some not. Though responsibility for the decline may be spread over the entire citizenry (either for what they did or what they didn't do), much of the blame for the harmful changes falls on leftists.

The America of The Greatest Generation has morphed into a nation being overrun by victims and takers. The Greatest Generation overcame the privations of the Depression and the drought and heat of the Dust Bowl years (in the 1930s, before global warming became the explanation for all atypical weather). They bravely fought European and Asian tyranny in World War II. They did their duty and, with their can-do attitude, contributed mightily to the establishment of America as a global power. That was then; this is now. Today, the America of the Greatest Generation is dying. Why did these changes occur? Is it possible to stop the decline? In this book, I will address some of the factors that are contributing to the decline of America and some of the consequences. Underpinning the decay are concepts rooted in misguided leftist policies, virulent anti-Americanism, rampant political correctness, and ideological environmentalism.

My maternal grandfather emigrated from central Europe as a young man at the turn of the 20th century. He learned the English language and became a US citizen. He worked his entire life in the seafood industry in Biloxi, MS and raised a family of 9 children. As my mother and her siblings were growing up, my grandfather forbade them to speak anything but English in the home with the admonition: "You are Americans and you will speak 'American.'"

The difference between my grandfather and many immigrants of today is that my grandfather *wanted* to become an American. He didn't want to be an Austrian citizen living in America. Today, many immigrants do not wish to assimilate into American culture. They want to be a Mexican or a Chechnyan or a Guatemalan living in America.

I had an uncle in the 4th Marine Division at the hell that was Iwo Jima in February of 1945, and an uncle in the US Navy who guided an LST (landing ship, tank) onto Omaha Beach during the Normandy invasion on The Longest Day (June 6, 1944). My father was also in the Navy and was a small cog in the massive invasions of Saipan and Okinawa. My Marine uncle, a 19-year old young man just months out of high school at the time, was severely wounded in the neck and shoulder by shrapnel from a Japanese mortar. He recovered after many months in hospitals. He eventually returned to Biloxi, married and had 3 children, but tragically succumbed in his 30s to a cancer that metastasized from his neck wounds.

All these men were proud Americans. Unlike Michelle Obama, they didn't have to wait until they were in their 40s to feel pride in America. My grandfather, uncles and father have now passed into the ages; may they rest peacefully. However, if they were alive today, they would be shocked by the things that are happening to America. When the "Day of Infamy" dawned, my uncles and father were ordinary young guys, just embarking on life's journey and looking forward to what lay ahead, when their lives were interrupted by war. America should be forever grateful for what they and their countrymen did between 1941 and 1945.

Some early American flags were emblazoned with the words "Don't Tread on Me." My father, uncles and their contemporaries saw to it that Japan and Germany learned that that phrase was no idle threat. The Japanese were particularly contemptuous of the fighting spirit of young American men in the 1940s. The Japanese soldier was taught and probably believed that American men were weak and pampered and would easily be defeated by the Bushido spirit of the Japanese fighting man. They eventually learned otherwise in savage, bloody fighting on numerous islands in the Pacific. Japan vastly underestimated the grim determination and rage of the American people engendered by the treacherous sucker punch they delivered on December 7, 1941.

The terrorist attacks on September 11, 2001 united America in much the same way that the "Day of Infamy" did in 1941. For a short while, the country came together in patriotic fervor. Regrettably, that unity dissipated within a few weeks. Sniping by leftists soon resumed and their vitriolic hatred for George W. Bush resurfaced. The left has blamed Bush for virtually everything that has gone wrong since the Jurassic Period. The squabbles and blaming Bush continue to this date, incredibly including the loss of lighting during the 2013 Super Bowl in New Orleans (1).

I was living in Singapore when the 9/11 attacks occurred, but I saw international news accounts of that dreadful day. I'll never forget going to church in Singapore that Sunday morning following the attacks. I can't remember anything about the homily that day, but I'll never forget what happened immediately afterward. Without any preliminary remarks and to the complete surprise to the largely Singaporean parishioners, the organist launched into a beautiful rendition of *The Star Spangled Banner*. It was an emotional moment and some of my fellow expats were moved to tears.

Also among my vivid memories of that terrible day was a news report showing jubilant Palestinians celebrating in the streets of Gaza during and after the attack. Of this I'm certain: That sorry Palestinian display disgusted and sickened many Americans and filled them with an angry resolve to exact justice for the thousands of innocent Americans killed on 9/11.

Thank God that the pantywaist Al Gore was not president in 2001! Most Americans were grateful that responsible adults were in charge. Though George W. Bush may have been inarticulate and I disagreed with of some of his policies, he was not only a good and decent man, but also a steadfast warrior when it came to fighting terrorism. Fortunately for America, he had surrounded himself with highly competent people, not the least of whom was Dick Cheney (certainly among the most capable VPs in the history of America, but you'd never know it based on the vicious attacks from the left). Advisers provided wise counsel and President Bush took decisive steps after 9/11. His administration protected the homeland from terrorist attacks over the remaining years of his presidency. That is indisputable.

Contrast the actions of the "misunderestimated" George W. Bush with those of President Barack Obama. Mr. Obama surrounded himself with amateurish ideologues and incompetents and his domestic and foreign policies have been inept. Clumsiness in foreign policies seems to be a hallmark of Democrat presidents, glaringly illustrated during the administrations of LBJ and Barack Obama. Yes, Obama authorized the strike that killed Osama bin Laden in Pakistan. It was a courageous decision for which Mr. Obama was deservedly praised by all Americans who wanted to avenge fellow citizens who perished on 9/11. However, on balance, Obama has been soft, and occasionally even apologetic, toward terrorists. As this book goes to press, it's been many months since the terrorist attacks in Benghazi in which Ambassador Stevens and 3 other Americans were killed and Mr. Obama is still covering up what happened and whatever culpability he may have had (see Chapter 5 and the Epilogue). By the time this book is published, will Mr. Obama have avenged the Americans killed in Benghazi? ...or will he simply ignore what happened as Clinton did after the killing of Americans in Mogadishu and the USS Cole attack?

Tactics espoused and taught by ultra-leftist Saul Alinsky in his *Rules for Radicals* (2) have been used to undermine America for more than 4 decades now. Alinsky was teaching community organizing when Obama was just a toddler. Though Alinsky employed use of what he called conflict tactics, some thought it more appropriate to label what he did "community agitating." Alinsky urged his acolytes to destroy the system *from within*. While he discouraged violence, it was not out of altruism. Rather, he thought that the objectives of radicals would be more readily achieved if they shunned use of bombings and killing. He believed that violence would alienate the masses of people (see Alinsky's discussion of "means and ends"). Alinsky suggested young radicals become *delegates* at political conventions, rather than simply fomenting unrest from the outside. He would surely have approved of the tactic of changing the system by getting elected to office, even if it required obfuscation and chicanery, hallmarks of Alinskyism. Practitioners of Alinskyism tend to be Machiavellian, socialistic and anti-capitalist. Unfortunately for America, Alinskyites succeeded beyond their wildest dreams. Notable modern day Alinskyites include Hillary Clinton and Barack Obama. Alinskyism will be discussed further in Chapter 2. But America's decline started long before Alinskyites came on the scene. The progressive administrations of Woodrow Wilson and Teddy Roosevelt mark a rational starting point (3).

It makes me melancholy to be so pessimistic about America and to witness its decline. Since the deterioration to this point required over a century, the final collapse into a full-fledged European-style Nanny State may require many more decades. It will likely continue piecemeal, such that the citizenry barely notices. Unless drastic shifts occur in the collective mindset, one day my grandchildren and great grandchildren will wake up to realize that America has decayed into just another second rate socialist country, like France. Indicators of decline are everywhere. Just to name a few:

- a lagging economy with pathetic growth rates,
- the country in near bankruptcy with a deficit of nearly $17 trillion (!),
- Standard & Poor's downgrade of the credit-rating for the US,
- emboldened terrorists (Benghazi, Algeria, Mali, Boston, etc.),

- ► socialistic programs (Obamacare),
- ► loss of world respect for the US ("leading from behind"),
- ► more Americans than ever (about 50 million) on food stamps
- ► high unemployment and underemployment,
- ► an imperial President who regularly skirts Congress and the Constitution,
- ► bureaucracies (EPA, IRS, etc.) that usurp Congress and infringe constitutional rights,
- ► out-of-control political correctness,
- ► purposeful obstruction of development of American natural resources.

Liberals, Conservatives and the Role of Government

Classical liberalism bears only superficial resemblance to modern liberalism, sometimes also called social liberalism. The "classical liberal" was for limited government, the free market, individual freedoms and opposed redistribution of wealth, much like the beliefs of what is today called a "conservative." In contrast, modern liberals favor a large, centrally controlled government (not unlike the government described by Orwell in 1984) capable of reining in its citizens such that societal perfection (social justice) can be imposed.

Liberals and conservatives have long disagreed about the role of government and this argument will continue long after we are all gone. In this book, I will name names of liberals that I believe have harmed America. It is my belief that the leftist philosophy of government has been a root cause of the decline of America for over than a century.

As noted previously, left and right have much different views on the optimal size of government. Conservatives typically believe that big government is the bane of the citizenry and that small government is more efficient (less costly) and less intrusive on individual liberties. In contrast, liberals are often dedicated social engineers who believe that government must provide for its citizens from womb-to-tomb, to right all wrongs and rectify all injustices. That inevitably results in a huge, bloated government. Many liberals believe that government should provide free food, free education, free health care, free housing, etc. Liberals appear to want an agency, a department or some other bureaucracy to regulate every conceivable human activity. Each time an inevitable tragedy occurs (whether caused by humankind or nature), they demand that new laws or regulations be enacted, regardless of whether relevant laws already exist.

Liberals occasionally pay lip service to what has been called "American exceptionalism" (4). However, more than a few leftists secretly despise America and take every opportunity to disparage the country and harp on its faults (5). There is no doubt that America has flaws and shameful episodes in its history. However, to my knowledge, not one leftist entertainer or Hollywood elitist has renounced his or her American citizenship and moved to a socialist paradise such as Cuba, China, Venezuela or North Korea. Nevertheless, I remain hopeful that Sean Penn, Bill Maher, Harry Belafonte, "Hanoi Jane" Fonda, Michael Moore, Janeane Garofalo, Susan Sarandon, Alec Baldwin and their ilk will soon move to Havana or Pyongyang. Not only would America be better off without them, the collective IQ of the country would go up. In recent times, more than a few liberals have expressed admiration for socialist demagogues who have been bitterly antagonistic toward America (Hugo Chavez, Fidel Castro, Joseph Stalin, Ho Chi Minh, Kim Jung Il, Mao Tse Tung, to name just a few). Even with its flaws, America remains a paragon of liberty in the modern world and the country that huge numbers of people from the 3rd World would prefer to be. How long that will continue is anyone's guess, given the behavior of leftists.

In contrast to modern liberals, conservatives typically believe in low taxes, individual liberties, a strong defense, personal responsibility and limited government—a government that doesn't try to regulate every possible human endeavor. For much of the past century, conservative ideals have been under assault by leftists. Typically, it's been done surreptitiously and incrementally. (Obamacare now, and later, a complete government takeover of the American healthcare system or, as it's known in Canada, socialized medicine.) While liberals want government to solve all of society's ills, conservatives are realistic enough to know that that is a pipe dream and that government can never be all things to all people. The more tax dollars the federal government takes in, the more it wastes, the larger and more bureaucratic it gets, and the more it encroaches upon the liberties of its citizens. With few exceptions, government tends to screw things up.

Conservatives differ from liberals in other ways. These differences will be discussed in greater detail in later chapters. However, for now, I should mention that conservatives are typically more pragmatic about government. Conservatives live in the real world and recognize that government can never solve all societal problems, but they know that government can become a serious obstacle to "life, liberty and the pursuit of happiness." Contrariwise, many leftists live in a fantasy world, dominated by phantasmagoric thoughts of utopia—a blissful world where all are equal, there is no injustice, and humanity lives in perfect harmony with Earth, all achieved through government. The concept of individual responsibility is foreign to liberals. To a liberal, no leftist is ever at fault for the misfortunes that befall them; it's always someone or something else that causes their failure or harm.

A principal constitutional task of American government is to provide for the common defense, but many liberals prefer to spend as little as possible on defense, so they can spend more to achieve social justice. Defense is one of the rare Departments where liberals wish to reduce spending. However, defense ("the military") is one of few government activities that work well.

Progressives/leftists believe in concentrating power in Washington DC. It was an unstated objective of both Teddy Roosevelt and Woodrow Wilson a century ago. Centralization was an underlying reason for many of their actions that set in motion leftist policies that are harming America to this day (3).

Obama's Contribution

As I write these words, America just re-elected a dedicated Alinskyite. Obama's re-election was a personal disappointment and this book is the result of an analysis of how such a person could twice be elected president. His re-election was an event symptomatic of the decline of America. He is an extreme leftist and an elitist demagogue who will do little or nothing to change trends. In fact, it is more likely that he will accelerate the decline. Mr. Obama will continue to spend profligately and, because of his incompetent anti-capitalist policies, the economy will spiral further downward. Thousands more jobs will be lost, though bureaucrats will continue to manipulate how unemployment is calculated to mask Obama's true impact on jobs. The long national nightmare of the Obama administration will continue until at least 2017. Having President Obama and his administration governing America is not unlike having a group of naive high school sophomores running the country. We will further discuss the ineptitude and corruption in President Obama's administration in Chapter 9. However, we will highlight here a few examples of Mr. Obama's contributions to the decline of America and what may be coming.

For most of 2012, gasoline cost between $3 and $4 per gal in America. It cost about $1.80/gal when Mr. Obama took office. Both Obama and Steven Chu, his former Energy Secretary for 4 years, would prefer it to be $8 per gal by the time Mr. Obama leaves office. Government resistance to developing domestic coal, oil and natural gas will insure that Americans continue to pay outrageous prices for gasoline. It will also result in additional losses of American jobs and raise prices for everything from the electricity for your home to the bread and milk you buy at the supermarket. For more than 3 years, Obama has fought the Keystone pipeline. His obstinate resistance to drilling on federal lands (*e.g.*, ANWR) is indicative of his contempt for the fossil fuels industries and for American security. Because Obama is less able to stop drilling on private lands, the oil and gas industries are booming in states like North Dakota.

The government will print more money (so-called quantitative easing), eventually leading to rampant inflation and causing the savings of senior citizens to wither. The cost of living will increase dramatically. Though the decline didn't start with Obama, he may be the proverbial "straw that broke the camel's back."

Jeremiah Wright was the pastor of the Trinity United Church of Christ in Chicago during the years Mr. Obama was a community organizer and an Illinois state senator. Wright was Obama's mentor and pastor for 20 years. I shall never forget Wright in a rant shouting "No, No, No! Not God bless America! God damn America!" Obama evidently sat in a pew and listened to Wright's hate-filled rhetoric all those years and said nothing in opposition. Like Reverend Wright, Mr. Obama detests America. However, while Wright can openly express his hatred, Obama must remain a closet hater of America. Though Mr. Obama can never say forthrightly how much he despises America, in a speech in Strasbourg, France shortly after he was inaugurated, Obama stated that "...America has shown arrogance and been dismissive, even derisive" (6). That speech was a disgusting attempt to ingratiate himself with the Euro states, some of which despise America. The fact is, Mr. Obama has only contempt for Middle Americans, saying in an unguarded moment that they "cling to their guns and religion" and "have antipathy" for those who are different from them. Like the dedicated socialist he is, Mr. Obama told Samuel Joseph Wurzelbacher, better known as Joe the Plumber, during his 2008 presidential campaign that he wanted to "spread the wealth around." How then, you ask, did he get re-elected? Good question, briefly addressed below and in greater detail in Chapter 3.

Rather than judging Mr. Obama solely by what he says, judge him also by what he has done. He has taken America further down the road to socialism, following a path blazoned by Teddy Roosevelt and Woodrow Wilson and propagated by Franklin Roosevelt and Lyndon Johnson. Obama has used executive orders, czars and recess appointments to implement dubious policies and to install ideologues who would never survive scrutiny by Congress. His actions have concentrated too much power in the Executive branch, contrary to the checks and balances intended by the constitution (7).

In addition to his cabinet appointments, President Obama has appointed numerous czars to oversee his leftist policies, more in 3 years than any previous president (8). However, Mr. Obama assigned formal titles that did not include the word "czar." This is another manifestation of his war on language (see Chapter 8) and an attempt to obfuscate. A comparison of the number of czars appointed by Mr. Obama relative to other presidents going back to Franklin Roosevelt is shown in Figure 1.1. The fewest czars were appointed by Republicans Eisenhower and Reagan (each appointed only 1 in 8 years) while Obama appointed 38 in 3 years. These czars are unaccountable and are not vetted by Congress. In some cases, they are clearly usurping the powers of cabinet secretaries. Few know how much they are paid and we know little about what they are doing, though Obama promised the most transparent administration in history.

Figure 1.1 "Czars" Appointed by Presidents
(1933-2012)

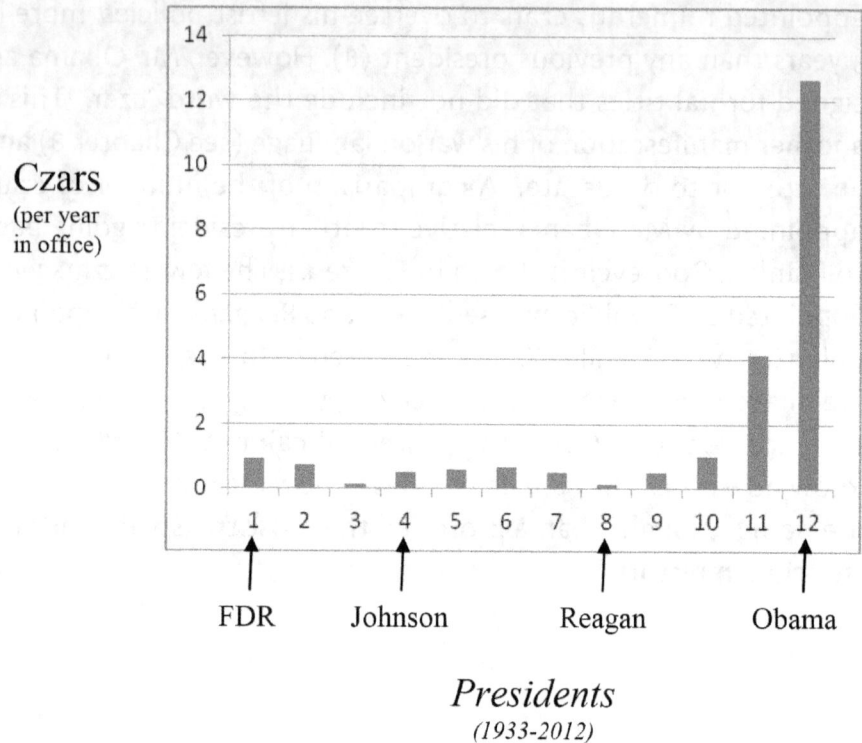

Czars
(per year
in office)

Presidents
(1933-2012)

Obama's most egregious damage to America will likely be done by his healthcare system, formally known as the Patient Protection and Affordable Care Act, but more commonly known as "Obamacare." Unfortunately, this act is far from affordable. He sneaked Obamacare through Congress using nearly every legislative expedient in the book, including a Senate vote on Christmas Eve. It will be hugely expensive, probably at least twofold the cost estimated by the Congressional Budget Office, and will require large tax increases. Bureaucrats are already busy writing thousands of rules. It may be the act that finally thrusts America into bankruptcy. The feckless Nancy Pelosi (D-CA) declared "we have to pass the bill to find out what's in it." Are you kidding me!? Since when does Congress pass a bill and read it later? The American people are beginning to see what is in the law and they don't like what they're seeing. They'll like it even less in 2014. Because Chief Justice John Roberts betrayed his conservative principles, the Supreme Court ruled (5 to 4) that Obamacare is constitutional.

Thanks to Justice Roberts, Obamacare is now the law of the land. Citizens are only beginning to feel the pain that Obamacare will inflict as it is fully implemented over the next few years. They are learning that Mr. Obama's assurances about reducing costs and being able to keep your existing plan and doctor were just a sales pitch. Though Mr. Obama promised premiums would go down, I just got a notice from my healthcare provider advising me that premiums are going up by about 17% in 2013. No telling how high they will be in 2014.

The Election of 2012

As the country approached election day in November 2012 with high unemployment, the huge deficit, the pathetic state of the economy, socialistic programs and the amateurish handling of foreign policy, I thought there was no way that the American people would be foolish enough to re-elect Mr. Obama. Unfortunately, I was terribly wrong. Clearly, I overestimated the intelligence of slightly more than half of the citizenry. I also failed to take into account the changing demographics of the US. (See Who Are Democrats? in Chapter 3.)

November 6, 2012 was indeed a sad, depressing day for conservative America. Mr. Obama was re-elected, insuring a continuation of leftist policies that will further the disintegration of America:

> ➢ President Obama will continue piling up enormous deficits. Long into the future, our grandchildren and great grandchildren will be paying for Mr. Obama's deficits.

> ➢ The administration will forge ahead with the socialistic

Obamacare plan.

➤ Mr. Obama will continue to persecute the fossil fuels industries in the name of "green energy" and stopping "global warming," much to the detriment of the economy and the American people.

➤ The Supreme Court will be stacked with extreme leftists like Ruth Bader Ginsburg. There's no telling what "The Supremes" will impose on the country or how long it will take to bring sanity back to the court.

➤ Joe Biden, a national embarrassment and quite possibly the most incompetent person ever to hold the office of Vice President, will continue as VP. Mr. Biden will continue committing one gaffe after another, unless he can somehow raise his IQ above that of an oyster.

➤ Electricity costs will skyrocket just as President Obama himself predicted.

Woe is me (and the US)!

President Obama was re-elected by his reliable base: a loose coalition of liberals, socialists, extreme leftists, Hispanics, African-Americans, union members, environmental activists, feminists, gays/lesbians/transgenders/bisexuals, Asian-Americans, and the clueless (aka the "moron vote"). Though small, the Jewish vote has historically gone >70% to the Democrat candidate and added to the coalition. Oblivious young people and indifferent white people also contributed. With the changing demographics, the leftist coalition will only become stronger in the future (see Chapters 3 and 10).

I actually thought that Mitt Romney was going to win in a landslide. Instead, we got the anti-capitalist, redistributionist Obama. How can America avoid further decline when it elects someone as vacuous and inexperienced as Mr. Obama? How could the American people reject an accomplished business man with a sterling record of achievement, a former successful governor from a nearly ungovernable liberal state, and a levelheaded man of integrity in favor of an inept, naive ideologue whose chief experience before his brief stay in the US Senate was as an inconsequential Alinskyite community organizer and an Illinois state senator (who usually voted "present" on controversial issues)? Romney would have rescued the country, at least temporarily, by providing competent leadership and restoring fiscal sanity to the Presidency. Instead, America has an ideologue determined to transform the country into a Nanny State and to spend the country into oblivion.

A few political commentators, including Bill O'Reilly, thought Obama was re-elected because he promised to give his supporters "stuff." If O'Reilly and other pundits are correct, just over half of the electorate simply voted for selfish gain (freebies) and were unconcerned that it would be harmful to the country. They will realize too late that much of what Obama promised is illusory or outright prevarications. Whatever the reasons, the unfortunate result is that the Obama administration will continue to damage the nation for several more years.

Is Mr. Obama purposely trying to destroy the country? I know there are those who believe that he is, but a slight majority is apparently inclined to give him the benefit of the doubt, or he wouldn't have been re-elected. Perhaps they think policies, such as Obamacare, obstructing the fossil fuels industries, and increasing taxes on the rich (in the interest of so-called fairness), are good for the country.

Some may view Mr. Obama's intentions as altruistic. He *appears* to be a good guy, sincere and compassionate. However, many like-minded Americans and I disagree with the way Mr. Obama is going about keeping his promise "to fundamentally transform" the country. Whatever his motivations, many of his ideas are extreme and simply wrongheaded.

The Mainstream Media

Historically, a free, independent and unbiased press has been an important part of the American republic. Among press responsibilities are to be skeptical of government, to serve as watchdogs for wrong-doing and "to speak truth to power." Unfortunately, those ideals have largely fallen by the wayside in recent years (except when a Republican is President). Ideally, journalists should put aside their prejudices and report evenhandedly, regardless of the party in power. Equanimity should be a hallmark of their reportage.

Fortunately, for much of its existence, America was the beneficiary of a fair press that largely lived up to its ideals. There are a few today who continue that tradition. However, beginning in the 1950s, a large segment of the mainstream media began to espouse the leftist agenda. It is that segment that I call "the mainstream media" and they must accept some responsibility for the country's deterioration, because they are simply not doing their jobs. Their performance has been abysmal. Today's mainstream media has degenerated into nothing more than a cheering squad for liberal policies and actions. They have become apologists for anyone or anything that promotes the leftist worldview. Perhaps it is true that Democrats don't actually own the mainstream media, but they do appear to have a long-term lease.

The leftist cheering squad is led by the print media, most prominently *The New York Times*, or, as I prefer to call it, the *Pravda* of America. However, chiming in are the television contributors, specifically NBC, ABC, CBS, CNN and, the most overtly leftist of them all, MSNBC. Over time, these have descended to reportage dedicated to the liberal agenda. One of the few sources of middle-of-the-road or conservative viewpoints in television is the Fox News Channel, which only came into existence in October of 1996. Previous to 1996, other than talk radio, only leftist versions of events were reported to the American public.

Journalists such as Maureen Dowd, Paul Krugman and Thomas Friedman, all of *The New York Times*, Eleanor Clift (of *Newsweek*) and

Jonathan Alter (formerly of *Newsweek*) regularly sing the praises of left-ists and liberal positions and trash anyone or anything conservative.

It is inarguable that there is a strong bias in the media in favor of liberal thought and it has been that way for a long time. Numerous studies have confirmed it. Nevertheless, some leftists continue to deny the blatantly obvious. But if you don't wish to take my word for it, you can experience it firsthand by watching a few minutes of the Chris Matthews or Rachel Maddow shows on MSNBC. (CAUTION: Common side-effects for conservatives include nausea, vomiting, headaches and extreme annoyance.)

Daily newspapers are in the throes of a transition that threatens their very existence. Many have either gone out of business complete-ly or scaled back to a few days per week. Other sources of information, such as the Internet and 24-hour cable news networks, are rendering daily newspapers superfluous. Moreover, the brazen leftist slant in their reportage has alienated many customers.

Journalistic malpractice committed by Jayson Blair (formerly of *The New York Times*) and Dan Rather (formerly of CBS News) caused a decrease in the already low esteem that the public held for journal-ists. TV journalism was further disgraced in 2012 when NBC *selectively* edited and repeatedly aired a 911 audiotape that made it appear that a man who killed a 17-year old African-American was a racist (9), though he was simply responding to a question from the 9-1-1 operator.

It is impossible to know how much of the disintegration of the country is attributable to liberal media bias. A few even suggest that liberal bias is not a large factor. I disagree. When citizens see only one view of events and it invariably favors the liberal cause, it can't be helpful to citizens who wish to cast an informed vote, not to mention whether it is fair to citizens who hold conservative views. If reporters would simply report the facts, there would be fewer issues. But too many try to shape public opinion toward their worldview. Dan Rather so hated George Bush that he had documents forged to damage Bush in a transparent attempt to have John Kerry elected in 2004.(Kerry as President? That's almost as scary as a Hillary Clinton Presidency!)

Would Obama have been elected and re-elected without the fawning coverage by the mainstream media? We'll never know. How many votes were cast for Obama because the media lauded Obama while simultaneously trashing Romney? Also unknowable. However, it seems that running for high elective office as a conservative is not unlike trying to win a football game with referees from the opposing team's coaching staff.

The mainstream media typically portray conservatives in the worst possible light. Conservatives for elective office are subjected to intense scrutiny by the media and liberal operatives, seeking to find anything, however trivial, that would discredit the candidate. It doesn't matter whether it happened 30 years ago, as long as it damages the conservative. Numerous case histories documenting leftist bias are provided by Bernard Goldberg (10-11) and Ann Coulter (12-14).

The mainstream media was guilty of gross negligence when they refused to vet Mr. Obama (twice). In 2012, we were told interminably about Romney transporting a kenneled dog on the roof of his car 30 or so years ago, but precious little about Obama's long-time friend, former Weatherman and terrorist Bill Ayers, or his America-hating pastor (and mentor) for 20 years, Jeremiah Wright. Aforementioned pundits Ann Coulter and former CBS reporter Bernard Goldberg, along with Sean Hannity, Mark Levin and Rush Limbaugh, have been outspoken about media bias. All are reviled by the mainstream media.

It's not only what the mainstream media do in presenting the news, it's also what they choose **NOT** to report. If a story is deemed damaging to a leftist cause, it may be ignored altogether or buried as a terse statement deep within the pages of *The New York Times*.

An occurrence during the final presidential debate in 2012 is a microcosm of mainstream media bias. The purportedly "unbiased moderator," Candy Crowley, sided with Obama and supported his contention that he had called the happenings in Benghazi a "terrorist attack" on the day after the attack. Whether Obama had, in fact, specifically called it a terrorist attack may be a matter of semantics and context. At the very least, Obama was disingenuous in one of his statements in the weeks after the attacks. That is, one of Obama's contradictory statements had to be an outright lie. Benghazi will be discussed further in Chapter 5.

In 2008, Mr. Obama claimed to have campaigned in "all 57 states." During a speech, Mr. Obama pronounced "corpsman" (a medic in military service) as "corpse man" more than once, so we know it wasn't simply a slip of the tongue. Obama's incorrect pronunciation did not get big play in the mainstream media, as they would have had Romney made them.

The mainstream media called Ronald Reagan dumb. George W. Bush and Dan Quayle were also said to be dumb (and worse). But Obama's VP Joe Biden can ask a paralyzed man confined to a wheelchair to stand up, or suggest to a largely African-American audience that Romney is going to "put y'all back in chains," or talk about the importance of "a three-letter word: J-O-B-S." Did Maureen Dowd or Jonathan Alter call Biden dumb for these remarks? Not a chance.

Do I fault Obama for misstating that there are 57 states or not knowing the commonly accepted pronunciation of corpsman? Do I fault Biden for asking a paralyzed man to stand up or to miscount the letters in a word? No, I don't. Everyone occasionally misspeaks, mispronounces a word or momentarily can't recall a well-known fact. It's human to err. We've all done it. That's not the point. It's the double standard about how such misstatements are reported by the mainstream media. It's the media gleefully ridiculing conservatives who misspeak, while remaining reticent about *faux pas* committed by Obama, Joe Biden and other leftists.

The damage being done to America has escalated over the past few years, nurtured by elitists in Hollywood, politicians in Washington, eggheads in academia, and the mainstream media. Bernard Goldberg wrote a book listing some of the people he believed "are screwing up America" (15). He wrote about the country's "tolerance of crap" and disturbing societal trends. It was no surprise to me that many on his list are liberals.

During reportage of the 2000 presidential election between George W. Bush and Al Gore, the mainstream media adopted use of the terms red and blue states. By tacit agreement, red was used to designate states that went Republican and blue for Democrat states. These conventions have now been accepted throughout the media and have become the standard in reporting election results. Have you ever wondered why the colors were assigned as they were? I have serious doubts that it was simply fortuitous. It is my suspicion that the decision was rooted in political considerations by the mainstream media. Red is the color usually associated with communism (see the 1981 movie *Reds* starring the well-known leftist, Warren Beatty). Since communism is an extreme leftist philosophy and most leftists reside in the Democrat party, it would have been perfectly logical to assign red to Democrat states. However, the media realized that anything remotely linking the Democrat Party to communism would be a losing proposition with many American voters. The politically astute move for the media was to assign red to the republican states, hiding behind the plausible (but phony) rationale that both begin with the letter "r."

I close this chapter with a story from World War II about the mainstream media of the mid-1940s. It offers a chance to ponder what might have happened had the media of today been there.

Late in the war, the Japanese had developed unmanned, hydrogen-filled (lighter-than-air) balloons equipped with devices capable of automatically controlling altitude and releasing bombs. Starting in November of 1944, they loaded thousands of these unguided weapons and launched them into the atmosphere to be swept eastward across the Pacific Ocean by the jet stream. The Japanese intent, of course, was to have the balloons deliver ordnance to the Pacific Northwest of the US to cause indiscriminant injuries, death and wildfires. Approximately 11% did indeed reach the US and Canada. When *Newsweek* ran a story about "mystery balloons" in its January 1, 1945 issue, the government subsequently asked the press not to write anything more about the balloons. Though the balloons did little real damage, the government was concerned that they could become more effective or could even be loaded with biological weapons, which they knew the Japanese had been developing for several years (16, Google "Unit 731" for more info). The government didn't want the Japanese to learn from press reports that some balloons had actually reached the US. The press of the 1940s complied fully and not a word was leaked. Only after 6 people in Oregon were killed by a balloon bomb on May 5, 1945, was the press released to write about the balloons in the interest of public safety. Because the Japanese assumed that the lack of news reports in the early part of 1945 indicated that the balloons were a failure, they stopped launching them. Can you imagine the press of today keeping such a secret? Neither can I.

Chapter 2

PROGRESSIVISM AND COMMUNISM

Karl Marx

Communism doesn't work because people like to own stuff.

Frank Zappa

Introduction

IN CHAPTER 1, WE MENTIONED changes that have occurred in America over the past century and harm inflicted by leftists, including a cursory look President Obama's "hope and change" contribution. We examined principal differences between liberals and conservatives and how the mainstream media has shirked its traditional role in recent times. Because they all think alike under their big tent, it matters little whether leftists are labeled liberals, progressives or socialists. Bolshevik, Menshevik and communist labels are usually reserved for those who are left of left. Though it is likely that liberals are reluctant to equate their ideas with the extremes of communism, they agree on many matters and both reside on the left side of the political spectrum. However, it's a near certainty that socialists and other leftists disagree on how to spend other people's money (1).

The history and ideologies of communism and progressivism have been subjects of encyclopedic discussions. Though enormously complex and broad topics, I will briefly outline what progressives and communists have done, and are doing, to America in this chapter. We will also survey what some well-known international communists and socialists have done after they seized power. This is certainly not to suggest that America will become like Pol Pot's Cambodia, but it is instructive to observe tactics used by leftists as they try to achieve utopia.

The vast majority of leftists call the Democrat party home. An analysis of the makeup of the Democrat Party is the subject of Chapter 3. Here, we'll trace the beginnings of the decline of America to policies established by Woodrow Wilson and Theodore Roosevelt during the so-called Progressive Era and have a look at damage inflicted by American communists.

We'll review the character assassination and verbal abuse that leftists and mainstream media from the 1950s heaped upon Senator Joseph McCarthy (R-WI). We'll also see that McCarthy was justified in his suspicions about widespread infiltration of communists in American government. Beginning in the 1990s, revelations from Soviet archives combined with declassified top secret US decrypts from the Venona program (2) vindicated McCarthy.

We'll briefly review how American communists infiltrated the Franklin Roosevelt and Harry Truman administrations, enabling top secret information to be funneled to the USSR. Revelations since the 1990s have shown beyond a shadow of a doubt that traitorous Americans inflicted damage on the US in the 1930s and 1940s. Yes, it was a long time ago; but it is worthwhile to review the behavior of leftists and media of the period, because there are lessons to be learned about modern leftists. In this regard, I am reminded of the well-known quote from philosopher George Santayana who admonished: *Those who cannot remember the past are condemned to repeat it.*

What's in a Name?

As previously mentioned, the Democrat party is home to most liberals. In recent times, many leftists shun the label "liberals." Apparently, Democrat candidates for elective office fear that liberal conjures negative thoughts in the minds of voters. Their concerns are well-founded, since more than a few conservatives think that many liberals are nothing more than closet socialists or even communists. Though it is true that not all leftist Democrats are socialists or communists, those on the far left are frequently the most vocal. It is also true that Democrats harboring any shred of conservative beliefs are endangered species, to wit, the so-called Blue Dog Democrats in the House of Representatives and Reagan Democrats. We'll discuss the Democrat Party in greater detail in Chapter 3.

Historically, people of the right have embraced the conservative label, without reservations. In contrast, many leftists resist being called names reflecting their political beliefs. Why is it a rarity when a leftist calls himself (or herself) a proud liberal?

In today's political parlance, many leftists prefer to be labeled progressives. Though some contend that there are differences (3), most do not differentiate. Because differences are subtle, I shall use the labels interchangeably. The label progressive has come full circle over the past century. It was very popular early in the 20th century (*The Progressive Era*). It fell into disfavor beginning in the late 1920s, but has regained popularity in recent times.

An organization called *No Labels* was established in 2010 and was formed to encourage bipartisanship. (Isn't the name *No Labels* a label?) Their mission statement is filled with Mom-and-apple-pie positions that would be difficult for anyone to oppose. However, *No Labels* avoids addressing controversial issues. George Will wrote an interesting editorial (4) entitled "The political fantasyland of the *No Labels* movement" in which he characterized the group's premise as preposterous. Though the *No Labels* organization doesn't take a stance on abortion, it would probably agree that leftists not be called liberals.

I am reminded by the *No Labels* crowd of Rodney King's inane question during the 1992 Los Angeles riots. Perhaps the *No Labels* organization should change its label to the "Can't-we-all-just-get–along-club."

The *No Labels* movement purports to be composed of Democrats, Republicans and independents, but it's clearly closer to the touchy, feely left. One of the co-founders was Nancy Jacobson (a "veteran Democratic fundraiser" [5]) and among the more prominent early members was the far left mayor of New York City, Michal Bloomberg (formerly a Democrat, then a RINO and now an independent). Some have noticed that there are far fewer conservatives in the movement. Regardless of the political persuasions of its founders and current members, it is an impotent organization that lacks a credible *raison d'être* and will probably fade away in the not–too-distant future. I intend to use labels throughout this book. It would be impossible to discuss the decline of America without labels, since it is my belief that leftists are primarily responsible.

Liberals probably think that the label "progressive" will convince people that they are forward-thinking. (Note the *Lean Forward* slogan used by the left-wing MSNBC.) Implicit in the progressive label is the unspoken idea that anyone who opposes them must be against progress. That is apparently how Mr. Obama in his 2012 campaign arrived at saying that Republicans are for dirty air and polluted water. Democrat operatives also ran a political ad showing Grandma in a wheel chair being thrown over a cliff by an evil Republican. While some liberals insist they be called progressives or some other name that obscures their true beliefs, they call Republicans vile names, including the pejorative "neoconservatives" (or neocons). Recall the despicable name (rhymes with stunt) that leftist comedian Bill Maher called Sarah Palin. Can you imagine the uproar that would have resulted if noted Libertarian comedian Dennis Miller had called Hillary Clinton that name?

Leftists call conservatives spiteful names, especially when losing arguments. All liberals can think to do is to shout their favorite epithet: *Racist!* Never mind that there are racists in all segments of society (whites, blacks, Hispanics, etc) and political parties (Democrats, Republicans, Libertarians, Greens, etc.). As we shall see, there are leftists who are virulently racist. Other names and adjectives that leftists favor for conservatives are:

- *fascists,*
- *bigots,*
- *extremists,*
- *homophobes,*
- *evil,*
- *stupid,*
- *Nazis,*
- *mean/mean-spirited,*
- *dumb,*
- *Neanderthals,*
- *troglodytes (or cavemen),*
- *primitives,*

and vulgar names derived from appearance, body shape or bodily functions. Recall how Clinton apologists like James Carville described Ken Starr and Paula Jones? Can't we all just get along?

Resorting to *ad hominem* attacks is a manifestation of the bank-ruptcy of ideas on the left. (Consider the title of Al Franken's book *Rush Limbaugh is a Big Fat Idiot* [6]). In the minds of many liberals, neocons are nothing more than gun-toting, bible-thumping, stupid white people from Middle America, otherwise known as flyover coun-try. Obama contemptuously described Middle Americans as people "clinging to their guns and religion," while addressing a liberal audi-ence in San Francisco during his 2008 campaign for the presidency. Unfortunately for America, a sufficient number of people "clinging to their guns and religion" voted for Obama in 2008 and helped re-elect him in 2012.

When liberals refer to Republicans as neocons, it is meant as an insult—an epithet not much different than the names mentioned above. "Righties" also indulge in name-calling, though the names in my judgment are less spiteful than those used by liberals. Use of "neo-commies" may be viewed as a fitting conservative response to being called neocons. Perhaps it is also appropriate for righties to call neo-communists who subscribe to Obama's socialist policies "Obamunists" (rhymes with communists).

Robert Bryce has written several books on energy and the environ-ment and I cite two (*Gusher of Lies* and *Power Hungry*) in Chapter 4 (7). Bryce is an outstanding author and an expert in matters related to energy. Though Bryce claims that he has no partisan agenda in *Gusher of Lies* (p 11), he refers to "warmongering neoconservatives" (p 10). Indeed, he devoted an entire chapter (*Gusher of Lies*, p 115) to what he called *The Neocon Crusade*. Notwithstanding his pejorative references to "neocons" (in *Gusher of Lies*) and "arch-conservative wingnuts" (in *Power Hungry*), Bryce is a rare liberal who truly under-stands the importance of fossil fuels and nuclear power to the future of America. (Bryce thoroughly debunked what he called the myths of "Green Energy" in *Power Hungry*.) Though I concur with his positions on energy (particularly his stance on ethanol), I must strongly disagree with his highly partisan characterizations of "neocons." Implying that all neoconservatives are warmongers is no more valid than suggesting that all liberals are pusillanimous pantywaists.

While on the subject of labels, let's consider what Peter Huber wrote in his book on the environment *Hard Green* (8), the subtitle of which was *Saving the Environment from the Environmentalists*. He wrote about the differences between what he called Hard Greens and Soft Greens. Huber's assessment of the Soft Green approach to environmentalism was as follows:

> *Soft Green is the realm of huge populations (molecules, particles) paired with the very weak (low probability) or slow (long time frame) effects. Soft Green is the Green of the invisible, the Green of the highly dispersed or the far future...*

Huber's long time frame phrase is particularly relevant to the controversy over global warming, because it may take hundreds or thousands of years to prove conclusively that the dire predictions of Al Gore and disciples are sheer claptrap.

I have been labeled (erroneously) a climate-change denier (CCD) because I do not accept that *humans* are causing the Earth to warm (9). In this book, I will often refer to ideological environmentalists who accept the global warming gospel according to Al Gore as global warming alarmists (GWA), a subset of what Huber labels Soft Greens. (The global warming boondoggle will be addressed in Chapter 6.)

In my estimation, George W. Bush demeaned conservativism when he ran for president by labeling himself a compassionate conservative. That label implies that everyday conservatives are not compassionate. Though I doubt that Bush purposely slighted conservatism, his use of that term suggests that he bought into the mainstream media's stereotyping of conservatives as insensitive and uncaring about the poor or less fortunate. Has any Democrat ever run as a "practical liberal" or a "small government progressive"? Such labels are, in fact, oxymoronic for Democrats, who are neither practical nor interested in limited government.

I will close this segment on labels with a few examples of spiteful quotes from celebrity leftists, as cited by Bernard Goldberg (10-12):

> <u>Janeane Garofalo</u>: *The Republican Party, their message and their politics of exclusion and the tilted playing field appeals to the dumb and the mean. There is no shortage of dumb and mean people in this culture. So therefore ... the dumb and the mean find a nice home in the GOP.*
>
> <u>Sean Penn</u>: *I am not disturbed by Ronald Reagan's Alzheimer's. You know, there's [sic] a lot cleaner pictures of karma in the world. I mean, it's not a very Christian way of thinking. I do stray sometimes. But I go from him mocking the farm workers and eating grapes on television during the boycott to him dribbling today. And I feel a sense of justice.*
>
> <u>Martin Sheen</u>: *George W. Bush is like a bad comic working the crowd, a moron, if you'll pardon the expression.*

The Progressive Era

The seeds of America's decline were sown during what has become known as *The Progressive Era*, the period roughly from the 1890s to the mid-1920s. It was a period of rampant liberalism and creeping socialism. America is dying today and the genesis of its illness may be plausibly traced to *The Progressive Era*. In many ways, today's mammoth American government had its origins in *The Progressive Era*. It encompassed the presidential terms of Theodore "Teddy" Roosevelt (R, 1901-09) and Woodrow Wilson (D, 1913-21). Though these men were from different parties, they shared a leftist vision of an Orwellian government that would be all things to all people. They expanded the reach of government by creating numerous federal agencies and usurping the roles of the Congress and the states. If the Constitution got in the way, they simply ignored it or amended it (13). Though the beginnings of what eventually became the Internal Revenue Service (IRS) date to the Civil War period, it was during *The Progressive Era* that the 16th Amendment was passed, formally authorizing the government to impose an income tax. The name IRS was not officially adopted until the 1950s. It was also during *The Progressive Era* that the 18th Amendment (Prohibition) was passed. Of course, the 18th amendment was later repealed (in 1933 by the 21st Amendment), but the entire period may be viewed as the beginning of government's attempt to control citizens' lives, something that continues to this day.

Though *The Progressive Era* brought about some warranted reforms and regulations, it was also responsible for heavy-handed regulations. As often happens, the pendulum swung from under-regulation to over-regulation, a trend that has been resurrected by President Obama. Regulations were clearly warranted in certain industries (*e.g.*, meat packing). Progressives reasoned that if new rules are good for meat-packing, then new rules will be good for other industries. This resulted in the implementation of regulations where they were ill-advised, for example, Prohibition.

Repeal of unwarranted laws and regulations is uncommon. It is more typical that, once put in place, laws remain for perpetuity. Today, burdensome regulations have become a barrier that businesses in America must daily overcome. Oppressive regulations make it very difficult for American businesses to compete internationally. Thousands of rules are imposed by clueless, unelected bureaucrats who have no accountability and little understanding of the real world, thanks in no small part to precedents established during *The Progressive Era*.

Many progressives of this era were firm believers in population control. The methods they favored included forced sterilizations and abortions. Their beliefs were influenced heavily by the teachings of Charles Darwin. They also accepted the comprehensively erroneous teachings of population doomsayer Thomas Malthus, the Paul R. Ehrlich of his era. Some progressives supported use of euthanasia or extermination to eliminate "the unfit," tactics that Adolf Hitler would employ in the 1930s and 1940s. As we shall see, noted leftists of the period such as Margaret Sanger, Teddy Roosevelt and Woodrow Wilson were steadfast believers in eugenics. In his insightful book *Merchants of Despair*, Robert Zubrin contended that the left betrayed its traditions and commitments when it began to embrace population control and Malthusianism in the late 1960s (14).

Shameful aspects of the progressive administrations of Teddy Roosevelt and Wilson tenures were their racism, their support of eugenics and their thinly veiled antipathy toward Catholics. Certainly since the turn of the 20th century, and perhaps even since the founding of America, Roosevelt and Wilson were the most racist persons ever to hold the office of President.

Consider the following Teddy Roosevelt statement (15):

> *Someday we will realize that the prime duty of a good citizen of the right type is to leave his blood behind him in the world and that we have no business to perpetuate citizens of the wrong type.*

Right type? Wrong type? Can you say bigotry?

Wilson was even more racist than Roosevelt (16). Though both Roosevelt and Wilson were defenders of eugenics, Wilson was somewhat less overt than Roosevelt. However, while governor of New Jersey, Wilson signed legislation that established *The Board of Examiners of Feebleminded, Epileptics, and Other Defectives,* allowing the state to determine whether procreation would be inadvisable for certain groups. For many progressives of the period, what they called the "lesser races" were among the groups for whom procreation was deemed inadvisable (17). Sounds like something out of Nazi Germany in the 1930s!

Margaret Sanger was a well-known activist, progressive and a pioneering feminist from the early part of the 20th century. Like Roosevelt, Wilson and other progressives of the period, she was an advocate of eugenics and wanted to eliminate what she called "the unfit." She is revered by modern liberals because, among her other progressive activities, she founded what today is known as Planned Parenthood, the largest U.S. provider of reproductive health services, including more than 300,000 abortions per year (18). The *Roe vs Wade* decision in 1973 by the Supreme Court has resulted in the abortion of more than *50 million* fetuses. Today's liberals and Planned Parenthood would probably prefer that the public not be reminded that Sanger, a progenitor of their movement, was an ardent supporter of eugenics.

There have been two political parties in American history dedicated to progressive principles. The first was *The Progressive Party* (also called *The Bull Moose Party*) under which Teddy Roosevelt ran in 1912. He came in second of 3 candidates, which essentially elected leftist Democrat Woodrow Wilson, who won only about 42% of the popular vote. The second was in 1948 when FDR's former Vice President Henry Wallace was the nominee of the so-called *United States Progressive Party of 1948*. The Communist Party of America (CPUSA) endorsed the left-leaning Wallace. However, Wallace won only 2.4% of the popular vote and no electoral votes and did not affect the overall outcome of the election. Truman was elected with just under 50% of the popular vote, but by a wide margin in the Electoral College. Though the 1912 Progressive Party and Wallace's Progressive Party of 1948 shared viewpoints on the role of government, there was no apparent connection other than their leftist philosophies.

Wallace was a single-term VP to Franklin Roosevelt and an admirer of leftist doctrines, including communism. FDR replaced Wallace with Truman for the 1944 campaign and threw a bone to Wallace by naming him Secretary of Commerce. Imagine how close Wallace, an Obama-type socialist, came to becoming president because of the death of Roosevelt in April of 1945. It would be another 64 years before America would have a president as dedicated to socialism as Wallace.

Damage by American Communists

For decades, America was harmed by communist espionage and interference in American domestic policies. It is distressing to note that a substantial portion of the damage was inflicted by American communists working for the USSR. Many were members of the CPUSA. Typically, these were idealistic leftist Americans thinking they were contributing to a better world by betraying America and helping the USSR, which they naively believed was the closest thing on Earth to utopia. Unfortunately, only a few defected to the USSR before they could harm America.

The administrations of Franklin Roosevelt and Harry Truman were both infested with numerous communist spies. These traitors to the US collected sensitive information and passed it to the Soviets, including knowhow about atomic bombs. In no small way, they enabled the Soviets to obtain The Bomb in 1949, years before they would otherwise have had it. Many of these traitors were exposed in the early 1950s by the House Un-American Activities Committee (HUAC) and Joseph McCarthy in the Senate.

McCarthy was viciously attacked by leftists as a loathsome, boorish demagogue. For decades, leftists bewailed the injustice of the hearings in which communists were outed. They declared the hearings a witch hunt. They loudly proclaimed that the accused were loyal Americans and were innocent of spying. The complicit media joined the denunciations of McCarthy and assailed anyone who supported McCarthy. (Sound familiar? Remember Ken Starr during the Clinton years and the vicious rants of the serpentine Democrat operative, James Carville?) Even today, leftists accuse anyone who dares question their loyalty guilty of McCarthyism.

Young American students today learn only the caricature of McCarthy as the heinous, repugnant senator who persecuted leftists. It is among the most flagrant examples of leftist bias in America's schools (to be discussed further in Chapter 8). It is confirmation that leftists with agendas write many of the texts used in high school and college today. It is an injustice that McCarthy's very name has become an epithet owing to the relentless attacks from the left. Interestingly, today's leftists and media often behave toward conservatives in the same contemptible ways that their progenitors did toward McCarthy in the 1950s. The deplorable treatment that the left inflicted on Robert

Bork and Clarence Thomas in the late 1980s and early 1990s is reminiscent of the way Joseph McCarthy was attacked in the 1950s.

Was McCarthy right 100% of the time? Of course not. For example, he was not correct about General George Marshall (19). Was McCarthy a flawed champion of his cause? Without a doubt (20). Though he may not have been right in all cases and some of his tactics may have been abrasive, it is clear from information that has become available since the early 1990s that he was correct far more often than not about communists infiltrating the US government.

Ann Coulter wrote poignantly about the legacy of Joseph McCarthy (21):

> *Despite the left's creation of a myth to defeat legitimate charges of treason, McCarthy had so badly stigmatized Communism his victory survived him. In his brief fiery ride across the landscape, Joe McCarthy bought America another thirty years. For this, he sacrificed his life, his reputation, his name. The left cut down a brave man, but not before the American people heard the truth.*

Unfortunately, the 30 years bought by McCarthy passed long ago. The left's relentless attacks on America resumed. Those who question the motives of the left are accused of McCarthyism. America continues to suffer the consequences.

Perhaps the most notorious communist spies during the McCarthy era were Alger Hiss (State Department), Harry Hopkins (a key adviser to Roosevelt) and Harry Dexter White (Treasury Department). All were in the Franklin Roosevelt administration and had access to top secret information. Even after Roosevelt was warned that Hiss was a Soviet spy, he ignored the warning and invited Hiss to accompany him as an adviser at the Yalta conference in February, 1945 (22). Is it simply a coincidence that Roosevelt acceded to Stalin's insistence that the USSR have hegemony in Eastern Europe? As a result, Poland and other eastern European countries spent more than 40 years in the orbit of communist USSR.

After the collapse of the USSR, archives of the former Soviet Union were opened and Venona decrypts (23-25) from the 1940s were declassified by the US in 1995. The list of *proven* spies included not only Hiss, Hopkins and White, but many others, including Julius and Ethel Rosenberg, who were executed as spies in 1953. For decades, leftists vociferously claimed that the Rosenbergs were innocent and were unjustly executed. However, between the Venona revelations, documents that became public after the demise of the USSR, and testimony from witnesses (such as former communists Whittaker Chambers and Elizabeth Bentley), it was proved unequivocally that both Ethel and Julius were traitors. Those sources also established that the influential journalist I.F. Stone was a communist agent/dupe who tried to slant American public opinion with his pro-Soviet writings. Stone could be considered the patron saint of many modern leftist journalists.

Since the collapse of the USSR, communism has been largely consigned to the dustbin of history, a fitting fate. The USSR was founded on Marxist-Leninist principles and treated its citizens with utter contempt. Ultimately, it crumbled from within. Russia's 70+ year experiment with Marxism cost tens of millions of lives and mercifully crashed in a heap in 1991. Its citizens were left with a depleted, despoiled country, still struggling today to join the 21st century. Misguided academics and leftists in the US continue to apologize for communism. They stubbornly contend that communism works, but was simply improperly administered by the Soviets. Is it working in Cuba? ...in North Korea?

Historians John Earl Haynes and Harvey Klehr spent years studying archives of the former KGB (opened to scrutiny after the collapse of the USSR) and declassified Venona messages. Together and separately, they have written eleven books dealing with the CPUSA during the 1930s and 1940s. One alarming trend they noted is that some of today's leftists in academia are writing revisionist history, portraying America as the villain and the USSR as the good guys in the Cold War (26, 27).

I lived the majority of my life during the so-called Cold War. Fortunately, it never turned hot, though there were several near misses.

Americans suffered a great deal of anxiety from the late 1940s until the USSR collapsed in 1991. Unfortunately, it is impossible to quantify the psychological damage and human cost of living under the threat of communist expansionism and nuclear annihilation by the USSR for more than 4 decades. However, there were proxy wars pitting America against communism. The two most costly were Korea in 1950-53 and Vietnam. Eisenhower sent a small contingent of advisors to Vietnam in the mid-1950s. America's commitment to Vietnam began to escalate in the early 1960s with the John Kennedy presidency and concluded (for America) during the presidency of Richard Nixon in 1973. Both the Soviets and Chinese communists played roles in these conflicts by providing materiel and/or manpower. For example, Soviet surface-to-air missiles were supplied to the North Vietnamese and cost many American lives. The Russians also provided pilots for the early jet fighters (MIGs) during the Korean conflict. The Chinese sent hundreds of thousands of troops over the Manchurian border into North Korea in late 1950 to kill Americans.

One of the great imponderables is: how many of the nearly 100,000 American deaths in the Korean and Vietnam conflicts might be attributable to spying by American traitors? Of course, it's impossible to know. However, based on documents that became available after the collapse of the USSR, Romerstein and Breindel (28) concluded that Stalin would *not* have allowed the North Korean communists to invade the South had he not had the atom bomb. If Romerstein and Breindel are correct, without information provided by American spies enabling the USSR to get the bomb years earlier, the Korean War might never have happened and nearly 40,000 Americans would not have died.

There is little doubt that spying on the US continues to this day, though most of the perpetrators are now probably spying for China and Iran and much of it is done in cyber space. Undoubtedly, Russia is also still spying on America.

I'll close this segment with a passage from Haynes and Klehr about the state of communism in the world today (29):

The Cold War is over and communism as an organized political force is dead. True, Communists still rule in the world's most populous nation as well as in Cuba and North Korea. But Chinese communism is an empty shell; its nominal ideology has less and less to do with the realities of China's economic and social life. Cuban communism awaits only the death of Fidel Castro for its implosion. And North Korea is a bizarre nightmare state, a living hell that has starved millions of its own citizens to death and crippled an entire generation of children through malnutrition. Communism as social fact is dead. But communism as a pleasant figment of the "progressive" worldview lives on, giving a phantom life to the illusions and historical distortions that sustained that murderous and oppressive ideology. The intellectual Cold War, alas, is not over. Academic revisionists who color the history of American communism in benign hues see their teaching and writing as the preparation of a new crop of radicals for the task of overthrowing American capitalism and its democratic constitutional order in the name of social justice and peace. Continuing to fight the Cold War in history, they intend to reverse the victory of the West and convince the next generation that the wrong side won and to prepare the way for a new struggle.

Neocommunism

Have you ever heard of neocommunism? I'm sure many readers have not, though the term has been around for years (30). But you've probably heard of neoconservatism in the most negative terms imaginable from the mainstream media. (There is little doubt that, if they comment at all, the media will denounce this book as racist neocon doggerel.) Though the remaining communist states may be hanging by a thread, communist precepts live on in the form of what may be called neocommunism. Like its predecessor, a key goal of neocommunism is to undermine America and its capitalist system.

Though neocommunism is rarely mentioned in the mainstream media, it is the new face of an old enemy of freedom-loving people everywhere. Since communism has largely failed, rebranding it neocommunism may be considered an attempt to fool people into believing it is something new and different. Though many citizens are unaware, its effects are widespread and it is changing the very fabric of America. It's a remnant of the Cold War but stays under the radar. It is an insidious, creeping mindset that is infiltrating every aspect of American culture. It permeates our schools, from kindergarten to the halls of our most prestigious universities. Most leftists won't call themselves neocommunists, preferring to use less inflammatory labels such as liberals or progressives. In some cases, people don't even realize that they are part of this pernicious development. But they are unwitting contributors to the demise of the American way of life. It is endemic in the mainstream media. Print media has a serious infestation of practitioners of the new communism. Unwitting neocommunists are also rife in the entertainment industry.

I briefly touched on Saul Alinsky in Chapter 1. Alinsky was a political guru to young idealists in the 1960s, a community organizer when Obama was still in diapers. Alinskyites could be regarded as the Menshevik wing of neocommunism. Though Alinsky passed away in 1972, students of his book *Rules for Radicals* are still around and actively working to bring down what Alinsky called the system. Alinsky taught conflict tactics, but also taught that radicals should work from *within the system*. He fomented class warfare by teaching the "Have-Nots" how to wrest power from the "Haves" and how to defeat the enemy (apparently, anyone to the right of Lenin on the political spectrum). For many years now, disciples of Alinsky have agitated by fanning "latent hostilities" (31) and tried to undermine the very country that allows them the freedom to do their work, actually using constitutional freedoms to secure what they believe is a better way to achieve utopia.

Perhaps you are unwittingly among the new communists. Answer the following questions:

> ➤ Do you think the rich are not paying their fair share of income taxes?
> ➤ Do you accept the assertion that America is responsible for the sorry state of the world?
> ➤ Do you believe that humankind is largely responsible for global warming?
> ➤ Did you ever vote for a candidate because a celebrity, such as Bruce Springsteen, Cher or Madonna, supported the candidate?
> ➤ Do you approve of the United Nations and believe it is a benign, non-political organization that is simply trying to improve the world?
> ➤ Did you buy an electric car or hybrid to "save the planet"?
> ➤ Are you opposed to drilling for oil in ANWR?
> ➤ Do you consciously avoid using certain words or phrases because you don't wish to offend someone or some category?

Did you answer "yes" to more than one question? If so, you might be a neocommunist. Interestingly, some who are not typically aligned with the left may have answered yes to some questions, because they have been indoctrinated (or brainwashed or duped) by the new communists. If you did so, don't feel badly. Many have been taken in by the arguments of neocommunists. New communists are very convincing and they are relentless. Part of their appeal is that they make people feel good about themselves. Who doesn't want to protect the Earth? You get to feel superior by opposing fracking or drilling, because leftists told you that natural gas and oil are dirty, disrupt the delicate environment, pollute the air and water and cause global warming.

It feels good to insist that the "evil" rich pay more in income taxes. If cool celebrity Bruce Springsteen supports Obama, they conclude that Obama must be right for the country.

Political correctness is a basic tenet of neocommunism. It is an attempt to control thought, a leftist concept intended to insure that no one in a protected group is offended by words or ideas. For example, neocommunists believe that it is less harmful to the psyche to refer to those who favor unrestricted abortion as pro-choice rather than pro-abortion. Who would want to be described as being in favor of destroying innocent fetuses? Who would favor aborting babies as they exit the birth canal using a practice euphemistically called "partial birth abortions," the details of which are too abhorrent to describe here? (Political correctness will be discussed further in Chapter 8).

Liberals think they know best how to spend your money and how you should live your life, right down to the light bulbs you can use in your house. They are disproportionately influential in many walks of life in America. They wield power in education, the workplace, and in local and national governments. They hold sway over many of the newspapers and other print media and the movie and entertainment industries. They are highly successful at shaping public opinion.

What Do Leftists Want?

Some suggest that leftists want power for power's sake. That is, they simply want to be "in charge" or to be the boss. Undoubtedly, that may true in a few cases. But I think far more regard power as a means to an end. They have adopted the Alinsky model on means and ends. Yes, they want to control the money, but I believe they care more about being able to dictate how you live your life: how many miles and where you can drive, how many kilowatt-hours of electricity you can use in your home (*Watch out for the thermostat police!*), what car you can drive, whether you can use plastic grocery bags or drink large sugary soft drinks, etc. Power provides them the platform from which they can dictate what people can and can't do, as they strive to achieve utopia.

Alinsky devoted an entire chapter in his *Rules for Radicals* to means and ends. He started by asking what he called the perennial question: Does the end justify the means? He then outlined eleven rules for what he called the ethics of means and ends. Alinsky writes: *To me ethics is doing what is best for the most* (32). Alinsky related a story about a confrontation with an unnamed corporation. During the episode, he was approached by a mid-range executive who disclosed that Alinsky's chief adversary from the corporation "preferred boys to girls." Though Alinsky rejected the offer in this instance, he admitted that if it had been necessary to win, he would have used the information that his chief adversary was homosexual. To Machiavellian leftists, everything is relative.

Liberals want to require that you do certain things for the greater good, if I may borrow a phrase from Hillary Clinton. This includes, for example, dictating what food or drink you can consume so that you won't become overweight or develop hypertension and burden the health care system.

Leftists have no concept of individual responsibility. When things go wrong, they are always victims. It's always someone else's fault that they can't succeed. It's because of George W. Bush, or Big Oil, or Big Pharma, or Wal-Mart, or Halliburton, or Bank of America, etc. It's the reason that they hurl invective toward conservatives. Indeed, some Democrat apologists, such as James Carville, have become rich distorting records of conservatives.

Leftists firmly believe that they are more intelligent than and are superior to the common man. Today, many Easterners and West Coasters feel that the center of the country is occupied only by ignorant dirt farmers, tobacco-chewing rednecks and unsophisticated NASCAR hicks and hayseeds. As the pusillanimous elitists and liberal snobs on the East and West coasts drink their lattés and sip their French wines, they speak condescendingly of the yokels from the interior of the country who disagree with their left-leaning philosophy.

If you happen to speak with a Midwestern or Southern accent, they assume you are stupid and/or bigoted. In their quest for utopia, they don't care if your freedoms get trampled.

Observe what has happened in San Francisco. I love San Francisco, though I didn't leave my heart there. What a beautiful city, blessed with gorgeous panoramic views and a year-round wonderful climate to have the misfortune to become a bastion of socialism. San Francisco is a perfect example of what happens when political correctness runs amuck, right down to dictating that what type of bag you must use for your groceries. Regrettably, Seattle, WA, Austin, TX and several other American cities are well on the way to becoming the San Francisco of their regions.

Liberals are not typically interested in equality of opportunities. Instead, they want equality of outcomes. They want everyone to be equal but, as in George Orwell's allegorical *Animal Farm*, some are "more equal than others." They want all citizens to have nearly equal amounts of money, even if that means taking income from the so-called rich and giving it to the poor like a modern day Robin Hood. Liberals believe that confiscatory income taxes on the rich are fair, but it's OK that nearly half of the population pays zero. As Obama famously told Samuel Joseph Wurzelbacher (aka Joe the Plumber) in an unguarded moment during the 2008 presidential campaign, government should "spread the wealth."

Though leftists wish to dictate what you can and cannot do, some believe that the same rules don't apply to them. For example, Al Gore has become a multimillionaire telling you that you must not drive an SUV and you must not use fossil fuels to heat and cool your home, both in the interest of stopping global warming. Meanwhile, Mr. Gore travels around the country in his private jet and limousine and uses huge amounts of electricity in his Tennessee mansion. What a hypocrite!! And don't give me that crap about Gore buying "carbon offsets" to compensate for his exorbitant lifestyle, as if planting a few palm trees in Malaysia will compensate for his profligacy.

What Do Leftists Do?

Leftists have been credited for doing much that has benefited Americans. According to Zubrin, *[t]he American left has a proud history of struggle to advance the human condition* (33). However, Zubrin erred when he credited Democrats with fighting slavery. As we shall see in Chapter 3, Democrats fought to preserve slavery and segregation (34). Clearly, I disagree with Zubrin about the contributions of leftism to America.

Notwithstanding the so-called proud history of the American left, Zubrin argued that the left betrayed its traditions and commitments when it embraced population control.

Over the past century, I'm certain that many American leftists have had the noblest of intentions to relieve suffering and to improve the human condition. Undoubtedly, many dearly love their families, are kind to their dogs and are sincere, patriotic Americans. However, substantial numbers have been brainwashed by the extreme left and are simply wrong about several contentious matters. They have been subsumed by radical, misguided zealots.

Despite the achievements of the left in America, *internationally* the left has a long history of contemptible behavior. Contrary to what you may have read in the history books, 20th century dictators Stalin, Mao *and Hitler* were all socialists, just cut from slightly different cloth. Leftists would like you to believe that Hitler was an extremist right-winger. However, Jonah Goldberg posits that Hitler was a "man of the left" (35). To Hitler, the state was supreme (just as in communism) and citizens must surrender liberties for the good of the state (36). Don't forget that the term *Nazis* was derived from the name of Hitler's political party: The National **Socialist** Workers Party. Remember also that leftists write most of the history books (37). While it's true that Hitler was virulently anti-communist, that was primarily because he thought he had a better brand of socialism, just as the Bolsheviks thought their communism was superior to that of the Mensheviks. Hitler had to eliminate communists because they were rivals to his effort to seize power in Germany.

What do American socialists have in common with Stalin and Mao? Perhaps only that they are leftists, are ardent believers in centrally controlled government and despise capitalism. In totalitarian countries, the state is everything; the citizen is nothing. To paraphrase the title from Hillary Clinton's book: *It Takes a Commune*. Ms. Clinton is also of the opinion that citizens must sacrifice "for the greater good."

Pol Pot and his Khmer Rouge communists committed horrible atrocities in the small southeast Asian country of Cambodia in the late 1970s. Pol Pot's henchmen tortured and killed more than a million Cambodians which at the time amounted to between 20 and 25% of the entire population of the country. (Think about that. It's as if 1 of every 4 residents of the Philadelphia area had been exterminated.) The Khmer Rouge executed the intelligentsia, doctors, nurses, landowners and anyone deemed to be a threat to their regime (38). They even killed people simply because they wore glasses since anyone wearing spectacles was regarded as bourgeois or an intellectual and untrustworthy (39).

The Killing Fields was an award-winning 1984 movie about Cambodia that was produced by liberals for liberals. Consequently, it adopts their usual anti-America slant and if you watch it, you have to endure their liberal Hollywood propaganda. Nonetheless, it is informative about the excesses of communism and depicts the brutality of the Khmer Rouge in the period 1975-79. Also, read *First, They Killed My Father* by Loung Ung (40), a book about the Pol Pot years in Cambodia, as seen through the eyes of a young girl who lived in Phnom Penh.

Similar atrocities occurred in Russia and China after communists took over. Joseph Stalin and Mao Tse Tung (sometimes transliterated as "Zedong") killed even more people than Hitler and his Nazi regime. History will never be able to count with certainty the number of people killed by Stalin and Mao, but it is undoubtedly in the *tens of millions*!

Observe what 50-60 years of uninterrupted communism has done in North Korea and Cuba. It converted those countries into virtual prisons. Both are among the most destitute, deprived countries in the modern world.

A remarkable photo of the Korean peninsula taken at night by a satellite shows the effects of 60+ years of communism relative to a free-market capitalistic system. The photo showed a darkened North above the 38th parallel, while the cities of the South were aglitter with lights. It vividly contrasts the dynamic capitalist economy of the South with the destitute communist North, which remains mired in a primitive existence because of communism. Since both sides are from the Korean culture, they are identical in all respects except the North has been under communist rule for more than 60 years.

Margaret Thatcher, The Iron Lady, passed away on April 8, 2013. She was a strong conservative, a magnificent leader and she virtually saved the United Kingdom in the 1980s. In a thoroughly disgraceful manner, leftists in England held a joyous street party flowing with Champaign to "celebrate" her death. They paraded in London with banners, some of which declared that the "witch" is dead. I know enough Brits to opine with that most would not approve of leftists rejoicing because of Ms. Thatcher's passing. The late Senator Edward (Ted) Kennedy (D-MA) was reviled by many conservatives in America because of his strident leftist views and despicable treatment of Clarence Thomas, Robert Bork and other conservatives. What might have been the level of disgust had the right celebrated in the streets when Kennedy passed away in 2009?

Chapter 3

THE DEMOCRAT PARTY

I am not a member of any organized political party — I am a Democrat.

Will Rogers

Introduction

THE DEMOCRAT PARTY IS THE party of liberals, progressives, socialists, and others from the left side of the political spectrum. It is my belief that flawed Democrat policies are largely responsible for a declining America, though nominal Republicans such as Theodore Roosevelt and Richard Nixon also bear some culpability. Starting early in the 20th century with Woodrow Wilson, Democrats set about converting Washington into a highly centralized, bureaucratic government and put the country on a path to socialism. However, I'm not suggesting a nefarious conspiracy by leftists over those many generations (save the communist activities discussed in the previous chapter). It's just that policies implemented in keeping with their fundamental beliefs led inevitably to the decay of the country. America went from being a land of self-starters with strong work ethics to a land overrun with victims and takers----a welfare state where it pays not to work. In more recent times, Democrats have fanned the flames of class warfare, continually pitting the poor against the rich, red states against blue states, women against men, "haves" against "have nots." They carp that the rich don't pay their fair share of income taxes. (However, in 2009 the top 10% of wage-earners paid about 70% of income taxes, the top 50% paid ~98% and nearly half paid nothing at all. Is that fair? See Chapter 7.) Aided by a complicit media, misguided academicians and clueless Hollywood elitists, Democrats have polarized the country. If the Union were a marriage, it would be said to have irreconcilable differences and headed for divorce.

In this chapter, we'll have a look at the make-up of today's Democrat Party and historic voting patterns and see how the changing demographics of America will impact the selection of future Presidents. We'll cite a few examples of the less than meritorious behavior of leftists and people from the party of the "little man."

Who Are Democrats?

Let me be clear, to borrow a phrase frequently uttered by President Obama: I am well aware that scoundrels reside in both major American political parties, though it appears to me that there are many more in the Democrat Party. The American public is bombarded daily with mainstream media stories about cretinous conservatives. Since Democrats and leftist operatives regularly excoriate Republicans, I will focus on Democrats in this chapter.

Regrettably, the Democrat party has been the dominant political force in American presidential politics since 1992. Democrats have won four of the last six presidential elections and one of the Republican victories was a real squeaker, requiring a ruling by the Supreme Court before finally being resolved in favor of the Republican. It's truly unbelievable, and in retrospect scary, to realize how close America came to having the hypocrite Al Gore as President.

Let's take a closer look at key constituencies of today's Democrat party (1). The modern Democrat Party is composed of a loose coalition of disparate groups:

- *liberals, progressives, leftists,*
- *union members,*
- *Hispanics (other than Cuban-Americans),*
- *African-Americans,*
- *Asian-Americans,*
- *feminist organizations (NOW, Code Pink, NARAL, etc.)*
- *pro-abortionists ("pro-choice") voters*
- *single women (married women usually vote Republican),*
- *gays, lesbians, transgenders and bisexuals,*
- *ideological environmentalists,*
- *Jewish voters,*
- *anarchists, anti-globalists and other malcontents,*
- *"moron voters" (defined below),*
- *disengaged, uncritical white people, and*

> ▸ *people who obstinately vote Democrat because of familial loyalty. (That is, they come from a long line of Democrats. To them, it's an inviolate "family tradition", to borrow a term from an old Hank Williams, Jr. tune.)*

These voting blocs, combined with demographic changes, have enormous implications for future elections which will be discussed below. However, it should be apparent that these groups, collectively, comprise a formidable obstacle to the election of any conservative.

Note that some factions of the Democrat coalition are from what the mainstream media call disaffected groups. While these groups may be disparate and have different leftist agendas, they are united in their disdain for anything conservative. For some liberals, it goes beyond contempt to hatred.

Of course, some factions in the Democrat coalition overlap. For example, most union members, leftist/progressives and moron voters are white. Consequently, it's not possible to determine the precise percentage of the US population in each of the voting blocs above. Furthermore, demographic data can be broken down into excruciating minutiae (Non-Hispanic-Native Hawaiian...). The big picture for the three largest demographic groups is approximately as follows:

a) White................72%
b) Hispanic 16%
c) African-American 12%

The figures above have been normalized using data from the 2010 census gathered from the Census Bureau web site (2).

American demographics have undergone huge changes in recent times. The percentage of whites in America has declined from about 87% in 1940 to around 72% today (see Figure 3.1), largely owing to the influx of millions of Hispanics from Mexico and Central America. In the 2012 election, whites comprised just 72% of voters. In 2012,

Democrats deceived enough independents and, along with their usual coalition, pushed their numbers above 50% in a sufficient number of states for Obama to win re-election. Nationwide, Obama won 51% of the popular vote, though he won handily in the Electoral College.

Figure 3.1 Whites in America
(1940-2010)

Source: en.wikipedia.org/wiki/White_American

Democrats get a disproportionate share of young voters (<25 years old). They also get a large portion of what I call the moron vote, to use a politically incorrect label, or what has also been called the "low information voter" (see Wikipedia article). In the context of voting, I define a moron voter as someone who is oblivious, and it is not only naive young people. They know embarrassingly little about the candidates or the consequences resulting from flawed policies. Numerous man-on-the-street interviews (Jay Leno, Sean Hannity, Jimmy Kimmel and others) have shown the shallowness and the pathetic lack of awareness that random citizens have of American history and basic civics. (See discussion about prohibiting the ignorant from voting in Chapter 7.) Many moron voters are also unfamiliar with the most elementary aspects of the US electoral process. They may not even know that the mentally challenged (to use the politically correct term) Joe Biden has been Vice President for years. They are likely unaware of Biden's numerous *faux pas*. However, they probably know that hip celebrities like David Letterman and Jon Stewart are Democrats. More than a few moron voters become Democrats for the rather superficial reason that they can be considered "cool." Hollywood elites, eggheads from academia and the mainstream media bombard the populace with the leftist mantra trying to influence the moron voter.

Democrats also get the bloc I call the cemetery vote. Large percentages of the deceased vote for Democrats (3). In the cesspool of Chicago politics from whence Obama emerged, the Democrat motto could be: *Vote early and vote often, even if you're dead.*

Though not identified as a separate voting bloc above, the "watermelon" vote goes largely to Democrats. Watermelons are a subset of what I identified as ideological environmentalists ----green on the outside, but red [communist] on the inside. Of course, not all environmentalists are watermelons. Indeed, though I am an environmentalist, I am definitely not a watermelon.

A recent estimate indicated that there are about 6 million Jews in the US (4). That number is at best a rough estimate. Jewish population in America has been declining in recent years because of low birth rates and intermarriage. Jewish people have historically voted in large numbers for Democrats. Why? I surmise a key reason is that Jews identify with the downtrodden and the Democrat party is <u>reputed</u> to be the party of the oppressed. Figure 3.2 shows Jewish voting percentages for Democrat presidential candidates between 1984 and 2012. On average for the period, the Jewish vote was about 74% for the Democrat candidate. President Obama received somewhat less than the average in 2012, probably because of his flagrant disrespect for conservative Israeli Prime Minister Benjamin Netanyahu and Obama's thinly veiled antipathy toward Israel.

Figure 3.2 Jewish Vote for Democrat Presidential Candidates

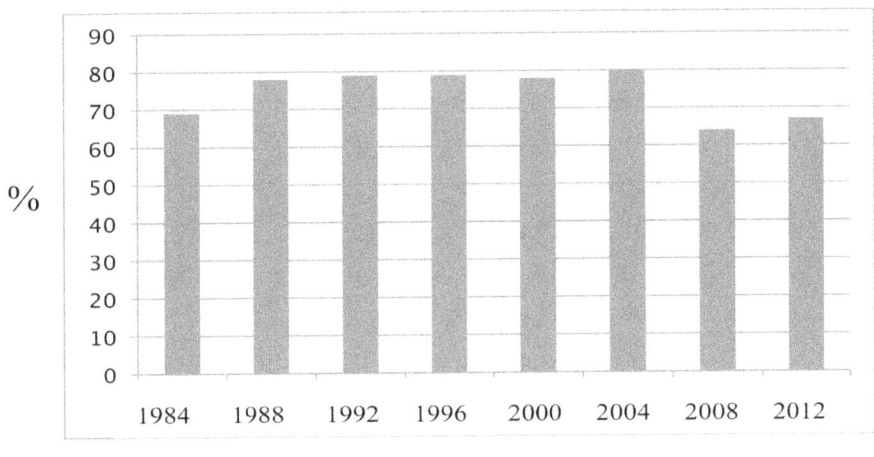

%

Year

Source: http://en.wikipedia.org/wiki/American_Jews

Consider the following hypothetical scenario for a presidential election that will take place in the not-too-distant future. For these calculations, we'll use the normalized 2010 Census Bureau figures for the major voting blocs above. For the moment, we'll ignore the smaller groups from the demographic mix and complexities introduced by the Electoral College. Let's assume that voting patterns from the recent election are replicated. If so, the Democrat can rely on receiving about 92% of the African-American vote and 71% of the Hispanic vote. (The African-American vote would go > 90% for the Democrat, even if Democrats were to nominate a ticket of Charles Manson and Jeffrey Dahmer.) When you go through the arithmetic, you find that the Democrat candidate needs less than 39% of the white vote to be elected (with 50.1% of the vote). It's actually worse than that for the Republican candidate, because I've not allowed anything for smaller groups that have historically voted in large numbers for Democrats (Asian-American, Jewish voters, to name a couple). It's abundantly clear that, unless the Democrat coalition unravels, it will be increasingly difficult for Republicans to win national elections in the latter half of the 21st century. In the not-too-distant future, it will be necessary for the Democrat to get only about one in three white votes to be elected. (See the analysis for 2052 and beyond in Chapter 10.) Based on demographic shifts and assuming voting tendencies remain unchanged, America will keep drifting leftward and the descent toward socialism will continue far into the future.

The Democrat Party is reputedly the party of the "little man," the party of the big tent, the party of society's downtrodden. It is purportedly the party of big hearts and compassion, the party of gentle, genteel people who want nothing more than a perfectly just society. You might think that, but you'd be wrong. The reality is quite different. Democrats display gentility only toward fellow leftists. How genteel were Democrat Senators in 1991 when they were considering Supreme Court nominee Clarence Thomas? Where was the renowned Democrat compassion? What Thomas endured during those hearings and the hostile treatment he received from Democrats are best recounted in Thomas's own words (5):

> ...I think something is dreadfully wrong with this country, when any person, any person in this free country would be subjected to this. This is not an opportunity to talk about difficult matters privately or in a closed environment. This is a circus. It's a national disgrace. And from my standpoint, as a black American, it is a high-tech lynching for uppity blacks who in any way deign to think for themselves, to do for themselves, to have different ideas, and it is a message that unless you kowtow to an old order, this is what will happen to you. You will be lynched, destroyed, caricatured by a committee of the U.S. Senate rather than hung from a tree.

Comparing his younger days in Georgia to what he was experiencing in his hearing, Thomas said: *I was starting to wonder if I'd been afraid of the wrong white people all along. My worst fears had come to pass not in Georgia but in Washington, D.C., where I was being pursued not by bigots in white robes but by left-wing zealots draped in flowing sanctimony (6).* How telling is that?! Democrat resistance toward the nomination of the eminently qualified Clarence Thomas was indeed a national disgrace, reminiscent of the way Democrats, led by the late Ted Kennedy, savaged the late Robert Bork in 1987.

Speaking of Bork, a speech by Senator Kennedy during the Bork hearings typifies the all-too-common liberal tendency to use hyperbole, distortions, character assassination and outright lies against conservatives:

> *Robert Bork's America is a land in which women would be forced into back-alley abortions, blacks would sit at segregated lunch counters, rogue police could break down citizens' doors in midnight raids, schoolchildren could not be taught about evolution, writers and artists could be censored at the whim of the Government, and the doors of the Federal courts would be shut on the fingers of millions of citizens for whom the judiciary is—and is often the only—protector of the individual rights that are the heart of our democracy ... President Reagan is still our president. But he should not be able to reach out from the muck of Irangate, reach into the muck of Watergate and impose his reactionary vision of the Constitution on the Supreme Court and the next generation of Americans. No justice would be better than this injustice.*

That diatribe was uttered by a person the Democrat Party proudly called the liberal lion of the Senate. Bork responded by saying that there was "not a line in that speech that was accurate" but to no avail. He was rejected 58-42 by the Senate.

Lest you conclude that the deplorable treatment of Thomas and Bork, which occurred in the late 1980s and early 1990s were aberrations, perish the thought. Democrats and sycophants in the mainstream media haven't mellowed one iota. One needs only consider the character assassination Democrats and their lapdog mainstream media committed against George W. Bush, Dick Cheney and Condoleeza Rice during the G. W. Bush presidency. Even today, after more than 4 years in office, President Obama and his comrades continue to blame everything that goes wrong on George W. Bush.

Dr. Condoleeza Rice is as gracious and accomplished an African-American woman who ever lived. However, to leftists she is first and foremost a conservative, and deserving only of contempt. Apparently, the Democrat concept of the ideal African-American woman includes current and former Democrat Congresswomen Maxine Waters, Cynthia McKinney, and the incredibly incompetent Sheila Jackson-Lee.

Rice was treated disgracefully by liberal Democrats during her senate hearing to be confirmed as Secretary of State in 2005. Senator Barbara Boxer (D-CA) was especially insulting. Condescending political cartoonists and liberal radio talk show hosts portrayed Rice as a compliant "Aunt Jemima" or worse. What happened to civility on the left?

More recently, consider the way the leftist media treated noted pediatric neurosurgeon Dr. Ben Carson, Herman Cain (Republican candidate for President) and former Florida Congressman Alan West. All were attacked simply because they are African-Americans who expressed conservative viewpoints. (Though Cain and West are Republicans, Dr. Carson characterized himself as a member of the "Logic Party.")

Philosophically, Democrats are not unlike the NAACP: They are in favor of advancement of African-Americans, as long as they are liberals. It's a form of racism that is endemic in the Democrat Party.

Another example of unseemly Democrat behavior is what Representative Alan Grayson (D-FL) did on the floor of the House of Representatives in 2009. Grayson was ranting about the Republican position on healthcare and displayed a flipchart on which was written the following statement: *If you get sick, America, the Republican health care plan is this: Die quickly.* For this and other outrageous behavior,

George Will characterized Grayson as "America's worst politician" (7). Unfortunately, such behavior by Democrat politicians has become almost commonplace. Even more reprehensible are the vile rants and name-calling of well-known Democrats Bill Maher, Janeane Garofalo and Sean Penn.

Early in the 21st century, it's perhaps difficult for people born since 1960 to grasp that, in the 1940s and 1950s, the Democrat Party was the party of segregation. They probably are also unaware that, prior to the Civil War, the Democrat party supported slavery. Nor is it likely that they are aware that the Democrat Party was the party of segregationist Bull Connor and the reviled Jim Crow laws (8). It was actually Lincoln and fellow Republicans that were largely responsible for passing the 13th Amendment abolishing slavery.

In campaigning for office, modern Democrats cannot say forthrightly what they really want or what they will do when elected. If they did, they'd rarely win an election. They must dodge, obfuscate, distort and lie. Just a couple of examples: Remember Obama's 2008 pledge to cut the deficit and to close the Guantanamo Bay prison immediately after being inaugurated? As I write these words in 2013, the deficit has soared to nearly $17 trillion and Guantanamo is still open. Have you ever noticed that placards and advertisements for Democrat candidates rarely list party affiliation? With few exceptions (e.g., Bernie Sanders of Vermont and Van Jones, Obama's former "Green Jobs" Czar), liberals don't openly admit to being Democrat, socialist or communist.

On the other hand, Mr. Obama did promise "to fundamentally transform" America. Disregarding the split infinitive (which may be grammatically incorrect but, for the moment, is not against federal law), that is one promise he kept. However, few Americans thought that he would try to turn America into France minus nuclear power. Democrats know that most Americans do not wish the US to become a European-style Nanny State. However, when Democrats are able to fool more than 50% of the electorate, the country gets incompetent leftist presidents such as Barack Obama and Jimmy Carter. In some cases, the Democrat needs only a simple plurality as in the elections of Woodrow Wilson and Bill Clinton. The coalition identified earlier in this chapter and their progenitors have been contributing to the destruction of America for a century. Though it may be possible to slow the decline, I fear the long-term damage is irreversible.

Democrats often blather about the unwillingness of Republicans to compromise. To a Democrat, compromise means giving them everything they want. Republicans recognize it, not as compromise, but as surrender. Now that Mr. Obama has been elected to a second term, he will use the presidential bully pulpit against Republicans even more. Mr. Obama no longer has to be concerned about being elected again (unless the 22nd Amendment that prevents a president from serving more than 2 terms is repealed). Consequently, he can give free rein to his socialist tendencies and it will be more of "my way or the highway" for Republicans, especially if Democrats win the House in 2014. Conservative Americans are in for a rough time for the next few years, owing to what will be done by the most leftist President ever to be elected. Unfortunately for conservatives, it is even more likely that extreme leftists will be elected in the second half of the 21st century (see Chapter 10).

America used to be a center right country. That has changed. America has evolved into a center left country. It will continue to shift leftward and will be dominated by the Democrat Party, which now controls the Presidency and the Senate. Today's America is being led by the party that venerates a former president who disgraced himself with a starstruck intern (in the Oval Office, no less) and lied about it under oath. That same party for many years championed as a liberal lion, a philandering senator who, in a drunken stupor, drove a car off a bridge leading to the death of a young woman.

There are few Democrats whom I believe are praiseworthy. Former Governor of Georgia and US Senator, Zell Miller, is at the top of my rather short list of Democrats worthy of respect. Miller, a true Son of the South, was born and raised in the mountains of North Georgia. A down-to-earth, common-sense, pragmatic man, a true rarity in the

Democrat Party, Miller held several views more consistent with conservatism. For example, as a public official he was a strong defender of 2nd Amendment gun rights. He favored low taxes, a strong defense and controlled spending (9-11). Despite these positions, he steadfastly rejected overtures to join the Republican Party, citing that he was "born a Democrat" (12).

Though I have great respect for Zell Miller, I must strongly disagree with his glowing praise for some of his fellow Democrats. He wrote admiringly of Senator Harry Reid (D-NV), Democrat operative James Carville (the bombastic ragin' Cajun), and the late Senator Robert Byrd (D-WV).

Senator Byrd was especially lauded in Miller's book (13). Miller called Byrd a great man and a legend. However, Miller was silent about Byrd's youthful participation in the Ku Klux Klan. Also, Miller said nothing about Byrd's use of the detestable term "white nigger" during a 2001 interview on race relations (for which Byrd later apologized). Miller's admiration of Byrd shows that even an intelligent, judicious man like Zell Miller can be horribly wrong. On the right, we do not perceive Byrd as praiseworthy.

Senator Miller's book *A National Party No More* proposes an idea that is diametrically opposed to what I suggest here. At the time he wrote (~2002), Miller thought the Democrat Party would have a difficult time winning national elections. In part, he based this belief upon his opinion that the Democrat Party erred in essentially writing off rural America and the South. Further, he thought it was suicidal to continue allowing the Iowa caucus and the New Hampshire primary to have such a large impact on the selection of the Democrat presidential candidate (14). He was particularly critical about labor unions wielding too much power in Iowa. Moreover, he believed the Democrat party was "being cannibalized" by special interest groups who care only about their narrow agendas.

While I certainly agree that the Democrat Party is being devoured by special interest groups, I do not share his belief that the Democrat Party will find it difficult to win future elections. Quite the contrary, I submit in this book that it is the Republicans that will have the more difficult time in the future. Since Senator Miller wrote his book, there have been three presidential elections and it's an unfortunate fact that Democrats won two of those. I rest my case.

Before leaving the topic of praiseworthy Democrats, I must say a few words about John F. Kennedy, the _second_ favorite President of all time for many Democrats (FDR is first). Perhaps Obama will eventually displace JFK or FDR in the pantheon of Democrat Presidents, but it's too early to tell. JFK was adored by the mainstream media and his every action was praised as if he were Zeus. We now know that there are many aspects of JFK that showed that he was an ordinary man with "feet of clay." However, JFK's character flaws are another story and beyond the purview of this book. Suffice it to say that JFK's performance during the 1962 Cuban missile crisis was masterful. Even if you have little respect for JFK because of his philandering and other misdeeds, you must acknowledge that his measured responses during that time of great peril very likely saved humanity from nuclear war. For that reason alone, JFK must be remembered as a Democrat worthy of respect.

Chapter 4

ENERGY AND THE ENVIRONMENT

If you don't know where you are going, you'll end up someplace else.

Yogi Berra

Fossil Fuels and Obama

OIL IS THE LIFEBLOOD OF the global economy. Without it, chaos would reign. Oil is essential for the quality of life enjoyed in the 21st century. Everyone is familiar with its refined products that fuel and lubricate our automobiles, trucks and aircraft. However, derivatives of oil cascade into many other aspects of your everyday life, from the tiles on your roof, to the tires on your car. Many might not realize that oil is also a crucial starting material for medicines, fertilizers and the billions of pounds of polymers that have become indispensable in modern life. The polyethylene bottle for milk in your refrigerator and the polypropylene fibers in your living room carpet are almost totally derived from petrochemicals. Despite the fervent hopes of Willie Nelson, Daryl Hannah and other biofuel proponents, there are now no *practical* substitutes for oil and it will remain an essential precursor for fuels and petrochemicals far into the future.

As suggested above, oil is enormously important in the transportation sector and is essential for myriad consumer products made from petrochemicals. However, oil is little used in America as a fuel for power plants (electricity generation). At this point, coal is the most important fuel for power plants (see Figure 4.1). This may change in the not-too-distant future for reasons we'll discuss below. Collectively, oil, natural gas and coal are known as fossil fuels and, as noted above, are critical to the modern way of life. However, fossil fuels have been targeted by the Obama administration and others from the left who blame fossil fuels for an incredible litany of humankind's environmental sins.

Figure 4.1 Fuels for Electricity Generation in the US*

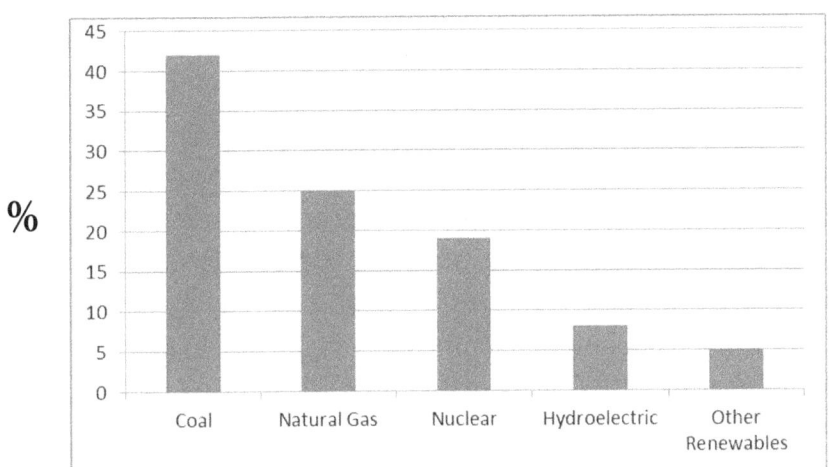

In 2011; oil was less than 1%. Source:www.eia.gov/energy_in_brief/article/ renewable_electricity.cfm

President Obama has waged a legislative war against oil. He consistently favors policies harmful to the oil industry and contrary to the best interests of the American people. For example, in January 2012 he rejected the Keystone XL pipeline thereby frittering away thousands of American jobs, not to mention losing a chance to secure a long-term source of crude oil for refineries in Texas. He has resisted drilling on federal lands (*e.g.*, ANWR) and off-shore. Little wonder that gasoline costs about twice as much as when took office!

Mr. Obama's resistance to developing domestic oil is tantamount to a hidden tax. It costs the farmer more to grow crops because prices have increased for his fertilizer and fuel to power his harvester and tractor. The trucker must pay more for diesel to transport the farmer's crops to market. The grocer must pay more for the delivered crops and raises his prices. Left holding the bag is John Q. Citizen who not only struggles to pay for the gasoline for his vehicle, but also sees his food costs go up, making it more difficult for him to feed his family.

Yet Obama can deceptively claim that these price increases weren't caused by him increasing taxes. A country that voluntarily refuses to develop its domestic resources does so at the peril of its economy and its security. It is not unlike committing economic *hara-kiri*, but that is precisely what the Obama administration appears to be doing.

Why is President Obama so hostile toward fossil fuel industries in America? In a nutshell (pun intended), he is beholden to the ideological environmentalist loons who helped elect him. In fact, President Obama could be said to be one of them. Apparently, ideological environmentalists want to return to "the good old days" when people lived off the land and internal combustion engines (ICE) didn't exist to pollute the air. Though Obama is against drilling for oil in the US, he has been very supportive of Brazil's plans to develop off shore oil. He offered Petrobras (the Brazilian petroleum company) $2 billion in loan subsidies for that purpose, while simultaneously obstructing offshore drilling in the US. Can you say hypocrisy?

America is being damaged by liberal activists trying to force the country away from fossil fuels. Bureaucrats and like-minded politicians are attempting to regulate the domestic oil, coal and natural gas industries out of existence. As suggested by the hidden tax discussion above, obstruction of the American fossil fuel industries is an anti-business policy that increases the cost of all goods for the consumer. Higher prices for fossil fuels cascade into increased prices for milk and bread at your local supermarket. Moreover, it imperils national security by making America more dependent on unreliable foreign countries (some of whom despise America). Though Obama wants green energy to become prevalent, it will not be possible anytime soon to use wind or solar energy to launch jet aircraft or to power an Abrams tank.

I recently read a post by a clueless blogger (probably a moron voter) who actually contended that carbon is evil. Perhaps he was just joking. However, some bloggers delight in berating and demonizing fossil fuel companies like BP and ExxonMobil (so-called "Big Oil"), in part, because they are major suppliers of evil carbon. The reality is that carbon is the element of life, the element that is the very basis of all organic chemistry. Without carbon, life as we know it would not be possible. We humans inhale air (composed primarily of nitrogen and oxygen) and exhale carbon dioxide (CO_2). Atmospheric CO_2 is essential to flora because it is the raw material for photosynthesis. Without carbon, there is no photosynthesis. Without photosynthesis, there are no plants. Without plants, there are no fauna, including humans.

Electric Cars and Hybrids

Consider the all electric cars of today. Despite what enthusiasts say, all electric cars are quite far from being ready for the big leagues. Nevertheless, we see Mr. Obama subsidizing them and doing everything in his power to make them successful. Even so, only rich movie stars and rock stars can afford a Tesla. At this point, few Americans want to buy Volts or Leafs (Leaves?). Electric cars are significantly more expensive than ICE cars and have limited range, even when fully charged. I might buy an electric car when they become more affordable, when their range is extended far beyond 80 or 90 miles, when the infrastructure for convenient recharging is in place and when recharging doesn't require many hours plugged into the grid. Today's electric cars are simply not practical for most of the car-buying public. In the interim, a hybrid is a practical alternative for those who feel compelled to reduce emissions and conserve gas. Though hybrids are more expensive than comparable ICE vehicles, they are viable and are here to stay. Contrariwise, the future of the all-electric car is very much in doubt. Electric cars will have a dubious future until deficiencies mentioned above are solved.

At this point, the all electric cars that many owners believe to be non-polluting are, in fact, being recharged primarily by power generated by burning of coal or natural gas. Bloggers argue interminably whether cars with ICE generate more carbon emissions than electric cars recharged with power from coal-burning utility plants. In my view, it's not unlike the meaningless arguments about how many angels will fit on the head of a pin. A few activists suggest that the argument may be moot, claiming that in the long run we'll get all our electricity from wind or solar. If that ever occurs, it will be in the distant future.

Power Plants

In recent years, nearly half (42-48%) of US electricity has come from power plants that burn coal. Natural gas accounted for another 20-25%. Hence, about two thirds of US electricity was generated using fossil fuels (see Figure 4.1). Oil accounts for very little of the fuels burned in power plants today, typically less than 1%.

Utility companies have begun a shift from coal to natural gas as fuel for generating electricity. There are a couple of basic reasons for this. First, natural gas has become available in abundance and is much less costly owing to the hydraulic fracturing ("fracking") and horizontal drilling revolutions. These technologies are enabling previously inaccessible natural gas to be extracted from the enormous deposits of shale in the US. Secondly, President Obama's EPA is forcing utility companies away from coal because of the cost of complying with environmental regulations. Imposition of punitive regulations on coal-burning power plants is one of the surreptitious ways that President Obama is forcing them out of business, as he pledged to do in 2008. Activists have apparently convinced Obama that fossil fuel industries are evil and should be punished for environmental transgressions. Ideologues evidently believe this will force the market toward what they believe to be more benign sources of energy. They care little that it will require consumers to pay much more for electricity.

A recent article in *Chemical & Engineering News* (the trade magazine of the American Chemical Society) cited a study that estimated the retrofitting of an average 400-MW coal-burning power plant will cost about $750 million just to comply with 2014 EPA rules (1). A separate study estimated that carbon capture and sequestration (CCS) would add about $200 million to the cost of a power plant (2). If accurate, these suggest that retrofitting a typical coal-burning power plant to become compliant with new EPA regulations and to be able to capture and sequester carbon will cost a total of nearly $1 billion. Moreover, CCS facilities are energy intensive and will consume about 25% of the output of the plant, *i.e.*, a 500-MW plant is effectively reduced to a 375-MW plant (2). Little wonder that President Obama said that his energy plan will make electricity bills necessarily skyrocket. These realities will make natural gas even more attractive as a fuel for new power plants.

Solar and wind energy are technologies that may *eventually* provide a significant portion of our needs, but they are not now ready for primetime. Moore and Shute opined that solar and wind power "are destined to have negligible impact on our energy challenges for at least two _decades_" (3, emphasis in original). I believe it will take much longer. Nevertheless, I sincerely hope that the cynical cliché is not correct: *Solar energy is the future of energy in America and always will be.* Like most reasonable people, I am hopeful that solar and wind will eventually be viable and not simply pie-in-the-sky solutions favored primarily by unkempt guys with straggly beards and devout vegans in sandals. We clearly need to continue research on these technologies. However, solar and wind energy will remain more expensive than energy derived from fossil fuels as far as the eye can see.

There is an additional disadvantage of wind and solar that proponents rarely mention. It is a major obstacle to wind and solar fulfilling a larger role in the future of energy supplies. To become truly competitive, both wind and solar energy must overcome the deficiency that they are not "always on" (4). The sun doesn't always shine, nor does the wind always blow. At this point, the intermittent nature of wind and solar energy would make a back-up plant necessary so that power can be supplied during down times (5). Thus, unless some unforeseen new technology for power storage is discovered, solar and wind power will have to be supplemented by plants using fossil fuels or nuclear reactors for the foreseeable future. This will necessarily introduce additional inefficiencies and waste causing wind and solar to become even more costly.

President Obama wants green solutions to the country's long-range energy problems. Though I join him in wanting green solutions, I think America should *quickly and aggressively* develop new domestic sources of oil and natural gas. We'll need these resources to bridge the time needed to develop viable, cost-effective green alternatives. I also believe that green solutions should succeed in the market place on their own merits. Apparently, President Obama doesn't care how much more green energy costs the American consumer. Unfortunately, Mr. Obama has provided ill-advised subsidies and loan guarantees to solar power companies. Several have already failed (most notably Solyndra) and cost American taxpayers hundreds of millions.

I believe it is wrong for government to mandate that Americans buy green energy. However, I fear such a requirement is in the offing by the Obama administration. Nor should our government try to steer the market toward green sources of energy by making it impossible for the coal, petroleum and natural gas industries to continue as viable businesses. President Obama is trying to drive fossil fuels industries out of business by imposing regulations, taxes or fees, and delaying (or outright denial) of drilling permits. Recall his rejection of the Keystone XL pipeline from western Canada to Texas and the prohibition of drilling in ANWR. A truly free market should determine which method provides energy at the lowest cost. By truly free, I mean a market unencumbered by government interference or mandates. Winners should be picked by the free market, not by government.

Natural gas burns much cleaner than coal and generates about 50% less carbon dioxide. Coal contains various amounts of sulfur, heavy metals (mercury, lead, etc.) and even small amounts of radioactive materials, while these contaminants are extremely low or non-existent in natural gas. When coal is combusted, small amounts of these contaminants are contained in by-product waste streams, either as flue gases or as solid waste (in the form of ash). These must be dealt with environmentally. In these respects, conversion from coal to natural gas for electricity generation is a positive for the environment. Because of the ongoing conversion to natural gas, President Obama's antithetical attitude toward coal will be among the less impactful outcomes of his crusade to destroy the fossil fuels industry. Eventually, however, America will need to develop its coal reserves, perhaps as a raw material for chemicals and synthetic fuels.

Nuclear Power

Nuclear energy is a clean, reliable, proven source of power for generating electricity. It produces no greenhouse gases. The hypocrisy of ideological environmentalists has been laid bare by their vehement opposition to nuclear power. This includes the NGOs (non-governmental organizations) purportedly dedicated to the environment, such as The Sierra Club, Greenpeace, The World Wildlife Fund, etc. If NGOs were truly concerned about stopping carbon dioxide emissions because of global warming they would embrace nuclear technology. The French generate more than 75% of their electricity from nuclear power. Well-designed and properly maintained nuclear power plants could literally provide energy for the US for *thousands* of years using the so-called fast-breeder reactors (6). Even French environmentalist Bruno Comby, who founded *Environmentalists for Nuclear Energy*, favors well-managed nuclear power plants because "nuclear energy is very clean, does not create polluting gases in the atmosphere, produces very little waste and does not contribute to the greenhouse effect" (7).

In addition to their fears of a meltdown (they are still reliving the Three Mile Island incident from 30+ years ago), NGOs find fault with nuclear power because of the waste it generates. Of course, waste disposal is a genuine problem, since some (not all) the nuclear waste may remain hazardous for thousands of years. However, viable solutions are available. The French have dealt with the waste problem safely since the 1960s. In America, the Yucca Flats, NV repository was an expensive, but safe and rational way, to deal with nuclear waste until Senator Harry Reid (D-NV) and President Obama succeeded in defunding (and effectively canceling) the project. Billions of taxpayer dollars have been wasted. The Government Accountability Office declared that the defunding was for *political reasons*, rather than for safety or technical concerns (8). In the meantime, nuclear wastes continue to accumulate at the locations where they are generated. This constitutes a much greater hazard to public health than storing the waste in a well-designed facility, such as the Yucca Flats Repository.

The Fracking Revolution

As indicated earlier, the natural gas industry has been revolutionized by fracking and horizontal drilling employed to extract gas from shale deposits (9). The fracking revolution began in about 2007 and the natural gas industry is now booming. Between 2007 and 2009, US reserves of natural gas rocketed by 35% (10)! Implications for America are potentially enormous. Previously, America was on a path to become a large *importer* of liquefied natural gas (LNG). Now, because of abundant, inexpensive natural gas from shale, America will probably become a leading *exporter* of LNG. (However, there is disagreement in the industry about the wisdom of exporting large amounts of American LNG, but that's another story.)

The fly in the fracking ointment is the resistance by environmental NGOs and activists that are fighting the technology, claiming that it harms the environment. A common complaint is that fracking causes ground water contamination. However, studies have shown contradictory results. Clearly, more research is needed to separate contamination caused by inadequate or lax procedures from contamination originating from natural sources. Whichever hypothesis is correct, *fix the problem*, but continue obtaining natural gas by fracking and horizontal drilling. It's vital to America's energy future.

It is entirely possible that there will be environmental impacts associated with fracking. However, that has been true as long as fossil fuels have been harvested by mankind. Just as we've done with oil, we must address such problems and develop techniques that minimize or eliminate them. It is important to recognize that *modern* fracking technology (as practiced in shale plays [11]) is in its infancy and, as it matures, better methods (12) will be developed and its environmental impact will lessen. With responsible companies, improved technologies, and, yes, even reasonable federal regulations, the abundant natural gas reserves locked in shale in the US may be claimed with negligible effect on the environment. This will be critical in long-range energy security of America.

My concern is that even after it has been shown conclusively that fracking is not the cause of ground water contamination and that fracking can be done safely with little impact on the environment, Neo-Luddite GWAs will continue to fight fracking. They will manufacture some other bogus claim (perhaps something like "it endangers the Kanab Ambersnail" or "fracking causes terminal halitosis"). To an environmental activist, it's a matter of principle to oppose any fossil fuel.

The US also has enormous reserves of coal. Indeed, coal is the fossil fuel that is presently the most prevalent fuel used to generate electricity, previously shown in Figure 4.1. Unfortunately, coal does not burn as cleanly as natural gas and releases more CO_2 into the atmosphere. President Obama despises coal, perhaps even more than he detests oil. He vowed to bankrupt the coal industry. The global warming loons object because of the warming that they claim CO_2 emissions cause. Though I don't discount that the world may be warming, I don't think it is caused by mankind's CO_2 emissions, nor is it an emergency that requires government to impose expensive, draconian (and ultimately, ineffective) measures to stop climate change. (Global warming will be discussed in Chapter 6.)

Prophets of Doom

Several books from decades ago have become bibles to ideological environmentalists. Among the more notable are *The Population Bomb* by Stanford Professor Paul R. Ehrlich and *The Limits to Growth* by the Club of Rome (COR). These books, published in 1968 and 1972, respectively, sounded alarms about overpopulation, limited resources and the environment. For example, doomsayer Ehrlich predicted that mankind would have devastating famines in the 1970s and 1980s during which _hundreds of millions_ would die of starvation. _The Limits of Growth_ predicted that humankind would run out of many critical natural resources, including oil, within a few decades. Though both have been shown to be comprehensively wrong, ideological environmentalists cling to their precepts to this date. They continue to claim that society will run out of food and resources, just later than Ehrlich and COR predicted. They also insist that America must convert to more environmentally benign sources of energy.

Amazingly, Ehrlich is still venerated by ideological environmentalists and has since become a tenured professor at Stanford. COR still exists, but has now shifted to doomsaying about climate change. The Cassandras from COR will probably be just as accurate about global warming as they were in their 1972 predictions about running out of natural resources.

Paul Ehrlich, the COR and other activists are members of a cabal that Zubrin called the antihuman movement. Antihumanism uses "inadvertent human damage to the environment as points of agitation to promote its fundamental thesis that human beings are pathogens whose activities need to be suppressed..." (13) The COR stated it even more bluntly: _The world has cancer and the cancer is man_ (14).

Another iconic publication to the antihumanist movement is Rachel Carson's _Silent Spring_, published in 1962. Zubrin praises Carson's book as a literary masterpiece, but he thoroughly dismantles the content of the book, which he exposed as "masterful propaganda" and a scientific "fraud" (15). Carson's book is largely responsible for the banning of DDT, a highly effective insecticide first used during WWII. DDT virtually obliterated mosquitoes that carry malaria and saved the lives of countless American servicemen. Because of the ban in 1972, Carson's misinformation and outright falsehoods have directly contributed to the loss of _millions_ of lives from malaria in the Third World. In effect, banning of DDT was a form of Malthusian population control. DDT was an early casualty of *The Precautionary Principle* (see Chapter 6), though it was long before antihumanists even came up with the term.

Conclusion

At the beginning of this chapter, I indicated that biofuels are not going to be viable substitutes for oil anytime soon. There is simply not enough arable land in the world to grow sufficient corn, soybeans, palm trees, etc. to replace the global requirements for oil. Also, technologies do not presently exist to enable these biomass feedstocks to be used for the vast array of other products derived from oil. Furthermore, unintended consequences caused by what Bryce called "the ethanol scam" (16) are rife. Perhaps the most heinous unintended consequence is the increased cost of food when huge quantities of corn are diverted into producing ethanol. The poor in developing countries are already living a meager existence and their struggles will be exacerbated by continuance of the ethanol scam. Like it or not, oil will remain a critical commodity for the global economy as far as the eye can see.

I have been a lifelong environmentalist---someone who has always held a deep appreciation for the wonders and beauty of the natural world. I have literally gotten my hands dirty planting hundreds of trees and shrubs over my many years. For more springs than I care to remember, I have planted a small vegetable garden. I will continue to do so, as long as I am able to till the soil. I have preserved resources and recycled whenever possible. Like most reasonable people, I want to conserve energy and preserve the environment for future generations. However, we must be realistic and recognize that fossil fuels are the only *practical* way we can bridge the gap between where we are now and where we want to be in the future. In the meantime, America must develop its own resources, including the vast quantities of natural gas that have recently become available from shale deposits. Looking beyond his soaring rhetoric, it is clear that President Obama is adamantly against development of domestic fossil fuels.

I close this chapter with a bit of wisdom from ex-Greenpeace member Bjørn Lomborg's book entitled *The Skeptical Environmentalist* (16):

> *In the longer run, it is likely that we will change from fossil fuels towards other and cheaper energy sources, maybe renewable, maybe fusion, maybe some as-of-now unimagined technology. Thus, just as the stone age did not end for a lack of stone, the oil age will eventually end but not for lack of oil. Rather, it will end because of the eventual availability of superior alternatives.*

Chapter 5

FOREIGN POLICY AND THE UNITED NATIONS

Many forms of Government have been tried, and will be tried in this world of sin and woe. No one pretends that democracy is perfect or all-wise. Indeed, it has been said that democracy is the worst form of government except all those other forms that have been tried from time to time.

Winston Churchill

Introduction

O VER THE PAST CENTURY, SEVERAL foreign policy decisions by liberal Presidents have cost many thousands of American lives and thrust America into wars, some justified, some not. It would require an encyclopedic discussion to cover the failings of Democrat presidents and that is beyond the scope of this book. Did conservative presidents blunder in foreign policies? Of course; even the magnificent Ronald Reagan made errors. But it was much more common for liberals in the White House to make bad decisions and their mistakes were far more costly. In this chapter, we will focus on actions taken by left-leaning Presidents and their consequences.

War is an ugly, brutal business that results in the tragic deaths and maiming of men in the flower of youth. Unfortunately, it is sometimes unavoidable.

Why do countries wage war? It is sometimes simply a means of self-preservation. However, there are many other motivations, a few of which are cited below:

- ➢ to seize land or natural resources by conquest (imperialism),
- ➢ to establish a new country (nationalism),
- ➢ to impose a political or religious system (e.g., communism instead of democracy or Islamic sharia law),
- ➢ to exact retribution for unprovoked attacks.

The origin of The First World War is usually attributed to the action of a zealous young member of the so-called "Black Hand" (a Serbian nationalist organization) who assassinated a crown Prince of Austria (Franz Ferdinand). This precipitated a sequence of events that escalated into WWI. As we shall see, FDR may have used devious means and overstepped powers granted to the Executive branch by the Constitution to project America into World War II.

We'll also briefly discuss the United Nations and how that international organization, established with such lofty goals after World War II, has deteriorated.

It Started with Wilson

The history of Democrat foreign policy decisions over the past century is fraught with instances of deceit, weakness and incompetence:

- ► After campaigning on a pledge to keep America out of WWI, Woodrow Wilson plunged the country into the European conflict in 1917. He instituted fascist measures in the name of fighting the war (1). While America had no choice but to fight in World War II, it seems that there was little justification for America entering World War I. Unfortunately, unresolved issues from WWI and the German hatred of the Treaty of Versailles led directly to World War II. In this respect, there were not two global wars in the 20th century, but only one which started in 1914, was temporarily halted in 1918, and began again in the 1930s.
- ► Jimmy Carter's timid leadership during the 1979-81 Iranian hostage crisis,
- ► Bill Clinton committed several blunders in the foreign policy arena:
    - o Clinton's cowardly withdrawal of US troops from Mogadishu, Somalia in 1993 in the aftermath of the Blackhawk Down incident, left the deaths of American soldiers and the barbaric desecration of their bodies unavenged,
    - o When he had opportunities to do so, Clinton declined to authorize taking out Osama bin Laden (well before 9/11),
    - o In response to the horrendous Al Qaeda bombings of two US embassies in Africa in 1998, he launched a few

      cruise missiles that fell innocuously in the Afghanistan wilderness and demolished a pharmaceutical factory in Sudan,

- o Clinton had essentially no response to the bombing of the USS Cole in Yemen in October of 2000, leaving it to his successor, George W. Bush, who decided to "stop swatting flies" but also took no specific action to avenge the USS Cole incident. However, Bush vowed to eliminate Al Qaeda (2) and his strong response after 9/11 kept the homeland safe for the remainder of his tenure in the White House.

FDR and WW II

The origins of World War II are complex (3) and, in many respects, are rooted in how the First World War ended. After World War I, a wave of isolationism swept the United States. Americans wanted no part of another European war, after witnessing the carnage of WWI. FDR campaigned for the presidency in 1940 promising to keep America out of the war in Europe. Nevertheless, he oversaw a selective service program in which, for the first time, the US had conscription during peacetime. He also implemented a program to support the British under the so-called Lend-Lease Act. Hundreds of American sailors and merchant marines were killed in attacks by the German Navy on US shipping in the North Atlantic during 1940-41, actually *before* the US was thrust into the war. The sardonic bromide of the time was that "England would fight to the last American."

      Some historians suggest that President Franklin Roosevelt schemed to force America into WWII (4), because he knew that Americans would never support entry into the war unless the US were to be attacked by an Axis power. Others insist that Roosevelt wanted to avoid war with Japan so that he could focus his efforts on defeating Hitler (5), whom he regarded as the greater danger to America. Was Roosevelt's intent to goad Germany and/or Japan into attacking? I tend to think the answer is probably yes, but I do not wish to discuss further the controversy over FDR's possible hidden agenda. It's a question best left to historians.

No matter your opinion on FDR's possible motives, it is fact that he took several steps in the late 1930s and right up to December of 1941 that could only be regarded as provocative toward Axis powers. For example, he froze Japanese assets in the US and imposed an embargo on sales of American oil to Japan because of their aggressions in China and Indochina (6). He urged that America become "the great arsenal of democracy" and, as previously noted, supplied war materiel to Great Britain, Russia and others under the Lend-Lease Act, which contravened the Neutrality Acts of the 1930s.

Oil was vitally important to Japan, which had no domestic sources. Roosevelt forced Japan to make a difficult choice—either it had to accept a humiliating withdrawal from China and Indochina (a course rendered virtually impossible by their Bushido culture) or move to capture the oil-rich countries of Southeast Asia. Japan chose war. To clear the way for their planned conquests, the Japanese thought that they needed to neutralize the American fleet in Hawai'i to give them freedom to invade Southeast Asia with minimal interference from the US. This decision led to the "day of infamy" attack on Pearl Harbor.

I certainly do not mean to suggest that FDR was wrong to confront the tyranny of Germany and Japan. FDR's methods may have been devious (depending upon your interpretations of his motives), but the Japan and Germany of those times were evil, imperialistic states that had to be confronted. World War II caused great pain in the US: America suffered more than one million total casualties, including about 292,000 combat deaths (7). However, World War II could be said to have had ultimate positive effects, because it marked the beginning of the US as a global superpower.

Undoubtedly, Roosevelt also considered other bellicose Japanese actions in the years well before the attack on Pearl Harbor. Japan's imperial tendencies were originally manifested as early as 1931 when they invaded Manchuria. They then attacked China. Horrific atrocities committed by the Japanese during their occupation of Nanking (now Nanjing) in 1937 shocked the world and were truly crimes against humanity (8). Japan also attacked the USS Panay on the Yangtze River in December of 1937, killing and wounding American sailors. In view of such aggressions, FDR was completely justified in his actions. With circumstances as they were in late 1941, war with Japan was virtually inevitable.

To reiterate, I do not fault Roosevelt for America's entry into WWII. It was an unavoidable evil dictated by the circumstances of the period. My dissatisfaction with FDR stemmed from his abuse of power demonstrated in both foreign and domestic policies. FDR was as close to a dictator that America has ever had. He overstepped powers granted to the presidency, allowing him to set in motion an expansion of government even beyond what Woodrow Wilson could achieve. As a result, the government has grown into the behemoth we have today. Jonah Goldberg even made a case that FDR, like Wilson before him, established a liberal fascistic state (9). By FDR's own admission, his New Deal domestic program had much in common with what Hitler and Stalin were doing in the 1930s (10). FDR's legacy is the gargantuan government that continues to expand even into the 21st century (11).

Today, President Obama appears to be trying to establish a similar imperial presidency using executive orders, czars and various agencies (EPA, IRS, etc.) to bypass Congress and govern by fiat.

Truman and Korea

Among the few steadfast foreign policy decisions made by a Democrat President was Harry Truman's response to the North Korean communists' invasion of South Korea in June of 1950. Though his initial response was firm, he later espoused a policy of stalemate, similar to what Lyndon Johnson did later in Vietnam. Ultimately, Truman's policy led to a "tie." The Korean peninsula remains a powder keg to this day, more than 60 years after a cease-fire (not a peace agreement) was signed. America suffered ~36,000 deaths and ~8000 missing in action. Technically, the two Koreas are still at war. Truman's policy in the Korean War (or "police action," as it was then called) was the beginning of limited warfare and restricted rules of engagement that later became a hallmark of the Vietnam debacle.

LBJ and Vietnam

Vietnam turned out to be a sorry chapter in American history. It polarized the country and could have had a different outcome with competent leadership in Washington. Lyndon Johnson and Robert McNamara were guilty of mishandling and micromanaging the Vietnam conflict, ultimately costing the lives of about 58,000 Americans. Though hindsight is always 20-20, there are many aspects of the Vietnam experience that should have been obvious, even to Johnson and McNamara in the 1960s.

It's difficult to win a war with one hand tied behind your back and when every important decision must be made by politicians and bureaucrats 12,000 miles away in Washington. US motives in Vietnam were noble, in keeping with John Kennedy's urging in 1961 for Americans to "bear any burden, oppose any foe, in the defense of liberty." In the minds of many young Americans, at least in the early and mid-60s, it was completely consistent with JFK's challenge to try to save the people of South Vietnam from the scourge of communism that the North Vietnamese were trying to impose upon the South. In the beginning, echoes of another famous JFK quote resounded in the ears of young American servicemen: "Ask not what your country can do for you, ask what you can do for your country." American idealism was soon to crumble, owing to the flawed policies of the Johnson administration and relentless pressure from the left, including many Democrats in Congress, to abandon South Vietnam, which eventually happened in 1975.

In the early 1960s, few Americans had even heard of Vietnam. Though origins of American participation in Vietnam went back to the few advisors sent by Eisenhower in the 1950s, things really didn't get hot for Americans until about 1965. However, the prosecution of the Vietnam War was horribly bungled. As noted above, the chief bunglers were Johnson and McNamara. What they required of young American servicemen was criminal. American pilots were sent to their deaths for inconsequential targets, such as tiny bridges in the jungle. On land, the tactic of "search and destroy" was adopted and cost many American lives. Americans were asked to fight and die for the taking or holding of an inconsequential hill, only to abandon it later. Statistics and body count became the measures of success on the battlefield.

Johnson would not allow pursuit of the enemy into Cambodia, thereby allowing the communists to retreat to their sanctuaries and regroup to return and kill more Americans. He would not allow invasion of the North. He greatly restricted bombing of Hanoi and Haiphong, the main seaport of North Vietnam. How can you fight a war when your leaders stack the rules of engagement against your own forces? The vaunted Ho Chi Minh trail would have been irrelevant had these targets not been off-limits. War materiel being sent down the trail would have been reduced to a trickle. These policies caused many unnecessary American (and Vietnamese) deaths and allowed the enemy to wage war long beyond when he otherwise might have.

It was only after Nixon authorized Linebacker II in December of 1972 that areas in and around Hanoi and Haiphong were relentlessly bombed. The so-called Christmas bombing brought the North Vietnamese back to the negotiating table and the war ended (for America) in January of 1973.

Even with LBJ's ridiculous restrictions, valiant American servicemen effectively won the Vietnam War in the field, but the war was lost in the streets of America. The 1968 Tet offensive was a catastrophe for the communists. True, they inflicted many casualties on American and South Vietnamese troops, but they suffered much greater losses (12). However, the media portrayed it as a defeat for the US and respected CBS newsman Walter Cronkite (a closet liberal) pronounced the war a stalemate. Street demonstrations in America, led by treasonous leftists waving Viet Cong flags in support of the communists, turned Tet from a victory into a defeat.

Mainstream media coverage of Vietnam was shameful. I believe many correspondents then were naïve leftists (as they are today) who sympathized with the communists in Vietnam and with the leftist protesters in America. If graphic pictures of the carnage in World War II had been shown (for example, from Normandy or Iwo Jima), I am certain that the American public would have been less supportive of the effort.

The treatment of Vietnam veterans upon return to the US was disgraceful. I put the blame squarely on the mainstream media and the extreme left-wing protesters who would spit upon men in uniform and call them "baby killers" and other vile names. Many veterans simply tried to blend into American society and kept their service a secret.

On March 31, Lyndon Johnson withdrew from the 1968 presidential race. Later that year, Richard Nixon was elected and took office in January of 1969. He began withdrawing US troops, and instituted a policy called Vietnamization, which effectively turned the war over to the South Vietnamese. A peace agreement was signed early in January of 1973 and direct American involvement in Vietnam essentially ended. In August of 1974, Nixon resigned because of the Watergate scandal. In the spring of 1975, in violation of the so-called peace agreement, the North Vietnamese communists launched a major offensive and overran the South. Because the Democrat-controlled Congress refused to fund actions to save South Vietnam, new US President Gerald Ford was unable to provide air support to help the South repel the communists. Despite the sacrifices of American servicemen over the previous decade, South Vietnam was lost. On April 23, 1975, Ford delivered a speech at Tulane University in New Orleans in which he said (13):

> *Today, America can regain the sense of pride that existed before Vietnam. But it cannot be achieved by refighting*

*a war that is finished as far as America is concerned. As
I see it, the time has come to look forward to an agenda
for the future, to unify, to bind up the Nation's wounds,
and to restore its health and its optimistic self-confidence.*

With these words, President Ford put Vietnam in America's rear view mirror. Shortly thereafter, the helicopter evacuation from the roof of the US embassy in Saigon (now Ho Chi Minh City) took place. Images of that humiliating withdrawal were burned into the collective memory of the American people. It brought a morose closure to the conflict so badly managed by LBJ.

Ronald Reagan and Lebanon

Ronald Reagan was despised by the left and regularly parodied and denigrated by Hollywood and the entertainment industry. For example, listen to Don Henley's otherwise beautiful 1989 tune *The End of the Innocence* for his not-so-subtle reference to "the tired old man that we elected king." Though I really liked Henley's music, he is a typical clueless entertainer in the mold of Bruce Springsteen and Madonna. Also, watch the offensive MTV video for Genesis' *Land of Confusion* which contains a disgusting parody of Reagan. Despite the left's attempts to destroy him, I believe that Reagan was the best President in my lifetime. However, I was disappointed in Reagan's tepid response to the 1983 bombing of the barracks in Beirut, in which 243 American servicemen (mostly Marines) were killed. It was not his finest hour.

In my view, the Beirut bombing could be regarded as the beginning of modern Islamic war of terrorism against America that continues to this day. If the Cold War is considered World War III, as many suggest, I agree with ex-CIA Director Frank Woolsey that the war on terrorism should be regarded as World War IV. Though it may be deemed to have started in 1983, it will continue far into the future. For many terrorists, only the complete destruction of America will end the carnage.

Reagan's withdrawal from Lebanon and subsequent actions were quite dissimilar to his firm response in 1986 after Libyans were found responsible for bombing a Berlin night club frequented by American servicemen. He ordered an air strike against Libyan targets and scared the bejabbers out of Gaddafi. Over time, Gaddafi became less antagonistic toward the US and eventually renounced his program to develop nuclear weapons.

Obama and the Attacks in Benghazi

The terrorist attacks on the American consulate and CIA station in Benghazi, Libya on September 11, 2012 are symptomatic of the deterioration of US foreign policy and the loss of international respect for America. It was what Michael Goodwin called (in an article in the September 16th edition of the *New York Post*) "the full flowering of a policy predicated on appeasement and apology" (14). Four Americans were killed, including Ambassador Christopher Stevens. Regrettably, the episode was politicized by Mr. Obama because of the impending presidential election. No doubt, books will soon be published about the attack in Benghazi. I just hope that they were written to tell the real story and not simply to exonerate President Obama. There were reports that Ambassador Stevens was tortured and raped before he was killed and his body dragged through the streets, reminiscent of the barbaric treatment of dead American soldiers by drug-crazed Somalis in Mogadishu in 1993. The sight of jubilant Somalis desecrating the bodies of dead US soldiers is seared in my memory.

For weeks after the Benghazi attack, Mr. Obama and his sycophants disingenuously claimed the attack was the result of a spontaneous demonstration over an anti-Muslim video that spiraled out of control. The Obama administration couldn't get its story straight and made several contradictory statements in the days and weeks after the attack. Obama himself declared numerous times in a speech at the UN on September 25, that it was caused by the video, though he knew well by then that it was not. Later, during the debates with Romney, he claimed that he had called the Benghazi event a terrorist attack during his Rose Garden statement on September 12th (and was backed up by the supposedly impartial Candy Crowley). In reality, he simply uttered the words "act of terror." In context, the remark appeared to be no more than a generic reference to terrorism rather than a specific characterization of the Benghazi attack as an act of terror. I can't help being reminded of Bill Clinton's semantic argument over the meaning of the word "is."

However, let's suppose for the purpose of discussion that President Obama specifically called the Benghazi attack an act of terrorism during his September 12th 2012 Rose Garden speech. If that is true, why did he send UN Ambassador Susan Rice to numerous Sunday morning talk shows on September 14th to say that the attacks were caused by the video? Indeed, why was the UN Ambassador sent to these shows in the first place rather than Secretary of State Hillary Clinton? Also, why did Obama himself make a speech at the UN on September 25th, still claiming that the attacks were caused by the video? Is Mr. Obama a blatant liar or is he simply incompetent? Mr. Obama's semantic contortions were enough to mollify his fawning media, at least temporarily. After the November election, Obama finally admitted that it was indeed a terrorist attack, which they had known on the day of the attack. He apparently didn't want anything that might contradict his pre-election narrative that he had defeated Al Qaeda (*Bin Laden is dead, GM is alive*, as VP Joe Biden gloated).

In retrospect, it is heart-rending to read about the pleas for help from Benghazi that were ignored, not only during the attack, but for weeks before. Who declined requests for better security and for help during the attack? Obama's obstinate stonewalling and glib explanations about the attack and whatever part he may have played are indicative of his duplicity and incompetence. All the while, apologists in the mainstream media either ignored the event or tried to provide cover for Obama. How can such a person be leading a superpower? How can such a country lead the free world?

Hillary Clinton, outgoing Secretary of State in the Obama administration, testified before the Senate in January of 2013 about the terrorist attacks in Benghazi. In classic Clinton style, she bobbed and weaved her way through the hearing. She obfuscated. She dodged. She became petulant during questioning, as if she were above being questioned by mere senators. She snapped indignantly "what difference" did it make whether the deaths of 4 Americans were caused by a terrorist attack or by a spontaneous demonstration that spiraled out-of-control. What arrogance! Ms. Clinton, perhaps it matters to the families of the dead Americans. Perhaps it matters to Americans who wish to know why its government lied for weeks afterward. Were the lies a cynical attempt to keep an incident that clearly showed the gross incompetence of the Obama administration from coming to light before the presidential election? Perhaps it matters who was responsible for declining to send help. Do Americans not have a right to know what happened and the culpability of Ms. Clinton and Mr. Obama? What if Richard Nixon had asked what difference did it make that a 3rd rate burglary was bungled at Watergate? Do you think the press of 1974 would have given Nixon a pass? Nor do I.

Even after 8 months, details of the Benghazi attack are still unknown and will probably not be fully understood until after this book has been published. We'll have to see whether Obama and his cronies are held to account for the debacle or the mainstream media will give them a pass. Isn't it reasonable to expect that all US facilities should have been put on high alert on the anniversary of September 11? Even more troubling are the conclusions that other terrorists will reach: that Obama's America is vulnerable to additional attacks and will do little to protect its citizens or to avenge such attacks.

Comparisons are being made between the Watergate scandal that brought Richard Nixon down in 1974 and the cover up of what went on in Benghazi, Libya on September 11, 2012. Though there are parallels, the events at Benghazi were far more serious than Watergate. To paraphrase Sheriff Buford T. Justice (played by the irascible Jackie Gleason) in the 1976 movie *Smoky and the Bandit*: "Watergate was baby shit compared to Benghazi." Watergate was a simple amateurish, botched burglary. Nixon was a fool to try to cover it up and ultimately paid a terrible price for his mistake. However, no one was killed in Watergate.

The Obama Administration and Egypt

Egyptian President Muhammad Morsi (a member of the Muslim Brotherhood) displayed his antipathy toward Israelis calling them "blood-suckers", "warmongers" and "descendants from pigs and apes" (15). He has also been quoted as saying: *We must never forget, brothers, to nurse our children and our grandchildren on hatred for them: for Zionists, for Jews* (16). The Obama administration provided F-16 jets and Abrams tanks to Morsi's military. I know these commitments were made long ago when Hosni Mubarak was president of Egypt. However, don't you think the Obama administration might have reconsidered, in view of the change in leadership and the animus expressed by Morsi toward Israel? This decision is effectively a betrayal of the historic US-Israel relationship. Will Israel, America's only true ally in the Middle East, pay a terrible price for Obama's incompetence?

United Nations

The United Nations was founded in 1945 to prevent wars by resolving international disagreements, to preserve human rights, to relieve human suffering and to promote friendly relations between nations. The following statements describe its objectives (17):

> ► *To maintain international peace and security, and to that end: to take effective collective measures for the prevention and removal of threats to the peace, and for the suppression of acts of aggression or other breaches of the peace, and to bring about by peaceful means, and in conformity with the principles of justice and international law, adjustment or settlement*

> *of international disputes or situations which might lead to a*
> *breach of the peace;*

> ▸ *To develop friendly relations among nations based on respect*
> *for the principle of equal rights and self-determination of*
> *peoples, and to take other appropriate measures to strengthen*
> *universal peace;*

> ▸ *To achieve international co-operation in solving international*
> *problems of an economic, social, cultural, or humanitarian*
> *character, and in promoting and encouraging respect for human*
> *rights and for fundamental freedoms for all without distinction*
> *as to race, sex, language, or religion; and*

> ▸ *To be a centre for harmonizing the actions of nations in the*
> *attainment of these common ends.*

The UN has several accomplishments in humanitarian missions to fight world hunger and disease. Eradication of the scourge of smallpox was a signal achievement. Another milestone in the history of the UN was the coalition assembled to confront the aggression of Saddam Hussein against Kuwait in 1990. UN troops (mostly American) also successfully fought the invasion by communist North Korea against the democratic South in 1950.

It is important to mention that the Kuwait defense was due, in no small part, to the considerable efforts of George H. W. Bush in assembling a broad international coalition. Also, the only reason that the UN could confront communist aggression in Korea in 1950 was because the USSR had had a temper tantrum and was boycotting sessions at the time. Consequently, the USSR was not present to exercise its veto power to prevent the UN from sending troops to resist North Korea's attempt to take over the South.

The UN has more typically shown itself to be an ineffectual organization in pursuit of misguided policies. The majestic ideals of the UN belie its hidden agenda. The United Nations often seems to be an anti-American, anti-Semitic, political organization. It has been used as a platform for third world despots and demagogues to harangue developed countries, trying to convince the world that developing countries are owed reparations. It has been used to persecute Israel. It is viewed by internationalists as the instrument through which they can achieve their vision of "world governance," as leftists Al Gore and former French President Jacques Chirac called it (18).

Of the 190+ member countries, the US pays the largest share (up to about 27%) of the cost of the UN. Nevertheless, the UN has morphed into an America-hating club for Third World countries, where the late Hugo Chavez of Venezuela could essentially call a US President the devil, on American soil, no less. Was Mr. Chavez really trying to develop "friendly relations between nations" (as stated in the 2nd UN objective) when he insulted George W. Bush at the podium of the General Assembly?

As mentioned in Chapter 4, the insecticide DDT was responsible for saving the lives of countless American servicemen during World War II. Recently, the UN took a formal position on DDT, effectively banning it completely by 2020. (The EPA banned DDT in the US in 1972.) The following is an excerpt from a recent analysis of the UN position on DDT (19):

> ... one might imagine that the United Nations would be working to secure the rights of sovereign nations to use the most appropriate public-health tools for their circum-stances. Regrettably, that is not the case. DDT use is not governed by a rational debate about its merits amongst relatively balanced, if opposing, interests but by vested interests opposed to its use. Far from being an impartial arbiter and defender of sound scientific evaluation in the debate over DDT, the UN is merely a conduit for anti-DDT interests.

For now, DDT is still permitted in exempted developing countries. Despite this, Reuters reports that malaria causes nearly a million deaths per year.

Like America itself, the UN has allowed itself to be manipulated by denizens of the left. The upcoming UN ban on DDT (20) is a misguided policy that will result in *millions* of deaths in Third World countries. In effect, the UN appears to be using disease as a means of Malthusian population control, a thinly veiled form of eugenics. Zubrin dedicated an entire chapter of his book *Merchants of Despair* (21) to the story of malaria and DDT. It was a sobering exposé of the truth about malaria and DDT.

The UN has become an organization seemingly dedicated to redistribution of global wealth. One of the ploys used by the UN to justify redistribution is to blame global warming on developed countries and to suggest that reparations should be made. In 1992 at the United Nations Conference on Environment and Development in Rio de Janiero, informally known as the Earth Summit, a treaty known as the Framework Convention on Climate Change (FCCC) was negotiated. The stated objective of the FCCC is to stabilize "greenhouse gas concentrations in the atmosphere at a level that would prevent dangerous anthropogenic interference with the climate system" (22). The Intergovernmental Panel on Climate Change (IPCC) was formed even before (1988) the FCCC treaty was negotiated. The IPCC now supports the FCCC by providing comprehensive scientific assessments of current scientific, technical and socio-economic information worldwide about the risk of climate change caused by human activity (23). The IPCC will be discussed in the context of the global warming boondoggle in the next chapter.

As previously noted, the UN is dedicated to population control. It attempts to achieve control through its United Nations Population Fund (originally the UN Fund for Population Activities or UNFPA). The UNFPA is an agency that has been accused by the Population Research Institute of using coercion and forced abortions as means of limiting population (24). Early 20th century progressive icon Margaret Sanger would be very pleased with the UNFPA. In part, the UNFPA justifies limiting population on the premise that fewer people will slow global climate change (25).

Not surprisingly, there is growing hostility toward the UN in America. Some of the more outspoken are clamoring for US withdrawal, or at least greatly reducing funding of the UN. US citizens are growing weary of paying a large share of the bills of an organization that appears to be a forum for bashing America. Also, many Americans do not wish to surrender sovereignty to the UN. Has the United Nations outlived its usefulness? In many ways, the answer is yes. It remains to be seen whether the UN will collapse, as did its impotent forerunner, The League of Nations.

Chapter 6

THE GLOBAL WARMING
BOONDOGGLE

We live in a society exquisitely dependent on science and technology, in which hardly anyone knows anything about science and technology.

Carl Sagan

Global Warming Alarmists

O VER THE PAST FEW YEARS on the southern fringe of the East Texas piney woods just northwest of Houston, we endured two winters during which there were a couple of unusually cold days where temperatures dropped into the teens (°F). I know readers from Wisconsin and Minnesota will scoff, since they are accustomed to much colder temperatures. However, temperatures in the teens are rare in southeast TX. I know it was colder than usual because several of my normally cold-hardy plants froze, including my queen palms and dwarf bottlebrush. As a chemist with more than 30 years in industrial R&D, I also know one should not invoke anecdotes as proof of a scientific trend. However, global warming alarmists (GWA) routinely suggest that virtually every unusual weather event is proof of global warming.

I reasonably attributed the frozen plants in my garden to the cyclical nature of weather. It didn't seem rational to suggest that we're entering a new ice age or that the unusually cold days were caused by global warming. Some winters are cold and some are mild. It's been that way for thousands of years and will be so far into the future.

Who are GWA? They are your neighbors and co-workers. They are in local and federal government (mostly Democrats, but with a sprinkling of misguided Republicans). They are teaching your children in school. They are in the mainstream media, the entertainment industry, the UN and many of our institutions of higher learning. John Brignell has ridiculed GWA with his hilarious list of the hundreds of things supposedly caused by global warming (1). In one respect, his list is humorous, but, in another, it is sad to realize that there are people who actually believe that global warming can cause so many implausible effects.

What does the controversy over global warming (or climate change as some prefer) have to do with a declining America? For one thing, trying to arrest climate change is a monumental waste of tax-payers' money at a time when the country is drowning in debt. The money will be wasted because we humans can no more stop Mother Earth from warming than we can stop a volcano from erupting or earthquakes from occurring. While we still need research to learn more about the complexities of climate, it is not an urgent matter, nor does it warrant the billions that are spent worldwide. Those billions would be spent much more wisely trying to find new antibiotics.

Global warming and cooling have occurred for time immemorial and will occur again. Permit me to use the well-worn cliché: "it's not a matter of if, but when." We humans will do what we've always done: Adapt. Sea levels will continue to rise, as they've been doing since the last Ice Age, which ended thousands of years ago. However, it will not happen overnight and we will move further inland. New York and Miami will not be inundated by rising sea levels any time soon, despite the scaremongering of Al Gore, preposterous Hollywood movies such as *The Day After Tomorrow* and numerous television documentaries (2) intended to scare the public into supporting draconian measures to combat climate change.

Many regulations that GWA and activists want governments to impose are impractical, utopian and/or anti-capitalist. They will be harmful to the American way of life. Enormous amounts have already been squandered and activists are clamoring that even more be spent. I realize that a few billion dollars is a pittance while President Obama is running trillion dollar deficits. But to quote the late Senator Everett Dirksen (R-IL) who facetiously observed about Washington's blasé attitude about spending: *A billion here, a billion there—pretty soon, you're talking real money.*

Measures that GWA want to impose on Americans in the interest of "saving the planet," will greatly increase the cost of living. However, it's not just the increased cost-of-living and the waste of taxpayer money. American living standards would deteriorate. By and large, Americans do not wish to live as if they were in a Third World country or like 19th century American frontiersmen. Rather, it's the Third World that wishes to live like Americans. We should do everything we can to lift up developing countries and help them achieve that dream, instead of asking Americans to regress. Free market capitalism, not socialism, is the system that affords the best chance for that to occur.

At this point, America is still a relatively free country. Here, GWA are free to act stupidly. It is their choice, though they shouldn't require stupidity from their fellow citizens. If effects for America were inconsequential, I would have no problem with GWA stubbornly wallowing in ignorance as long as they didn't fritter away enormous amounts of taxpayer dollars, or take away my freedom to choose incandescent light bulbs, or to have a rib eye steak for dinner. Should government mandate that citizens purchase a certain percentage of electricity from more expensive green sources (wind or solar) or dictate the thermostat setting in your house? Of course not. Unfortunately, we may be heading in that direction.

To paraphrase the immortal words of Rhett Butler in *Gone with the Wind*: "Frankly, my dear, I wouldn't give a damn about GWA if they didn't insist that government enact laws to stop climate change." Good intentions notwithstanding, such laws will be ineffectual. Unfortunately, the Obama administration has bought into the GWA fallacies about climate change. Burdensome, unnecessary regulations will be enacted, much to the detriment of America.

An interesting case history, though not directly related to the climate change controversy, may be revelatory as to how local governments might try to micromanage climate. A few years ago, San Francisco's response to what was essentially a citizen littering issue may be suggestive of what may be coming. The SF Board of Supervisors banned plastic grocery bags (made from polyethylene) in part because they were said to cause eyesores in the community and occupy an inordinate amount of space in landfills (3). It is a near certainty that local governments will pass similar regulations to stop global warming, though GWA would probably prefer that the *federal* government pass the laws. In any case, it will be futile. In a few years, global cooling will commence and mankind will not be able to stop it either. However, liberals will undoubtedly claim more taxes are needed to prevent the calamity of global cooling, just as they did in the 1970s.

Since the problem of global warming is worldwide, activists may insist that the only way to proceed is under the auspices of the United Nations, an entity that appears to be dedicated to the subjugation of America, as suggested in Chapter 5. Surrendering sovereignty to the United Nations is not in the best interests of America. Imposition of carbon taxes to "save the earth" is another boondoggle, an excuse by internationalists to punish the US and redistribute wealth.

Global warming has become a *cause célèbre* among watermelons, though *anthropogenic* global warming may go down in history as the biggest scientific hoax since the Piltdown Man fiasco early in the 20th century. Watermelons come from all walks of life, a few famous, but most are not. Some are highly intelligent people who are otherwise quite rational. It is not possible to provide a comprehensive list of persons responsible for the global warming hype. Suffice it to name just a few of the more vocal, some of whom you may recognize:

- ▶ Al Gore (former senator and VP),
- ▶ Laurie David (wife of comedian Larry David, producer of *Seinfeld*),
- ▶ Heidi Cullen (formerly chief GWA at the Weather Channel)
- ▶ James Hansen (Head of NASA's Goddard Institute for Space Studies),
- ▶ Leonardo DiCaprio (Hollywood actor and environmental activist)
- ▶ Michael Oppenheimer (Princeton University professor) and
- ▶ Bill McGuire (British volcanologist and doomsayer extraordinaire).

These GWA and their comrades from academia, the mainstream media, government and Hollywood, along with thousands of anonymous acolytes, work tirelessly to convince the world that mankind is responsible for Earth overheating and that governments must do something *urgently* to stop a global climate calamity. Some are anti-technology Neo-Luddites (see discussion of *The Precautionary Principle*, below).

Not so long ago (the 1970s), activists were telling us that we were on the verge of a new ice age. For example, Stephen Schneider, the late environmental biologist, suggested in 1971 that a new ice age might be triggered by man's pollution. Schneider retracted his ice age projection in 1974, and, before he passed away in 2010, had turned 180° and transformed himself into a GWA.

Stanford Professor Paul R. Ehrlich has been widely, and deservedly, ridiculed for the risible predictions made in his apocalyptic 1968 book *The Population Bomb*. Professor Ehrlich, who made David Horowitz's list of most dangerous academics ([4], also see chapter 7), was a global cooling alarmist in the 1970s and, like Schneider, pivoted to become a global warming alarmist. (Paul R. Ehrlich of Stanford should not be confused with Nobel laureate Paul Ehrlich, who helped develop the germ theory of disease [5]).

An editorial in *The Times Picayune* of New Orleans on November 8, 2012 is illustrative of the mainstream media's tendency to attribute atypical weather events to global warming. Bob Marshall wrote an op-ed that was titled: *After Sandy, there's no denying global warming.* Sandy was the category 1 hurricane that struck northern New Jersey on October 29, 2012. Though Sandy was assuredly a tragic occurrence and caused widespread miseries for people in the Northeast, it was most certainly NOT caused by global warming. Rather, Sandy was caused by a rare confluence of meteorological circumstances. Unusual, yes; unprecedented, no. *Eighty four* hurricanes and tropical storms have hit the northeast since the 17th century (6). Was global warming to blame for the devastating hurricane that struck New England in 1938?

GWA often suggest that only urgent action will "save the planet." They urge that we act quickly before we reach the tipping point, which they claim looms just over the horizon. Often, it is downplayed or not mentioned at all that citizens will need to reduce use of fossil fuels. Activists would prefer that people return to the days of living off the land. They apparently want transportation to be achieved by horse and buggy or bicycles. Perhaps they will demand use of cow dung for heating and cooking, as in the Old West. Actually, some GWA want to eliminate cattle altogether because bovine flatulence liberates too much methane, which is more than 20 times more potent than carbon dioxide as a greenhouse gas. If GWA get their way, you can kiss your favorite steak goodbye. Ah, "the good old days": outhouses, no cars, no electricity, no rib eye or filet mignon steaks, horse crap in the streets, etc. I don't know about you, but I do not wish to live like a 19th century frontiersman.

Anyone who disagrees with GWA is labeled a "climate change denier" (or worse) and equated with holocaust deniers. (I guess the GWA don't subscribe to the *No Labels* movement.) GWA are a pestilence on America. They accept the hogwash put out by James Hansen and Al Gore. They want to convince the American public that we must raise taxes and submit to the UN to solve the impending climate catastrophe. Not only do GWA want Americans to take measures that will lower standards of living, they also favor actions that will dramatically increase the cost-of-living. They have even tried to indoctrinate the very young in our schools, using the gospel according to Al Gore to scare the bejabbers out of grade-schoolers. If we don't do something RIGHT NOW, we're all going to die!

There is a maxim that came into vogue many years ago, but is still used when pondering why certain things occur in politics. In the 1976 movie about Watergate (*All the President's Men*), the character called Deep Throat told Woodward to "follow the money." That could well apply to the funding of research on global warming. If *anthropogenic* global warming were to be exposed as the boondoggle it is and it were widely known that warming has occurred many times in the past (Google *Medieval Warm Period*, for example), many GWA would no longer be able to feed at the public trough. GWA scientists benefiting from government largesse would stop and they would have to find other sources of research funding. The billion dollar gravy train would grind to a halt. That is why GWA react so viciously and attack anyone who is skeptical about *human-caused* global warming.

In 1988, the United Nations established the Intergovernmental Panel on Climate Change (IPCC). The declared mission of the IPCC is "to provide comprehensive scientific assessments of current scientific, technical and socio-economic information worldwide about the risk of climate change caused by human activity..." (7) Of course, this statement has as its underlying premise that humankind is indeed causing climate change.

The IPCC is comprised of hundreds of scientists, experts, politicians and bureaucrats, all nominated by the governments of member countries. Many are environmental activists, economists, sociologists and other occupations having little to do with climate science (8). The IPCC is composed of three Working Groups (9). Working Group 1 deals with the scientific basis of anthropogenic climate change. Unquestionably, there are accomplished climate scientists in the IPCC and they have provided thoughtful, valuable scientific contributions to IPCC reports (10). However, they are much less involved in the writing of the *Summary for Policymakers* and are sometimes ignored altogether if their work contradicts IPCC positions that warming is out-of-control and humans are responsible.

Like the UN in general, the IPCC is essentially a political organization. Bureaucrats, activists and politicians write much of the *Summary for Policymakers* portion of the IPCC reports, the part that is most widely read. They have been known to edit the summary to include statements not necessarily supported by scientists. Contrary to accepted scientific principles in which one draws conclusions *after* an hypothesis is formulated and data are collected to test that hypothesis, the IPCC *starts* with the conclusion that humankind is causing global warming.

The *undeclared* mission of the IPCC is to redistribute as much wealth as they can from the US and other advanced countries to the Third World, all in the name of saving the planet. Third World countries continue to clamor for developed countries to compensate them for global warming damage. Such payments are nothing more than reparations---a socialistic wealth transfer to compensate for perceived past crimes against Mother Earth. Do you think the IPCC would ever proclaim the truth that climate is beyond the ability of man to control? ...that developed countries are not responsible for global warming? Never! That would in effect put them out of business.

GWA frequently state that the "science is settled" and those who disagree are heretics. As Al Gore is wont to say with a dismissive wave of his arm "The debate is over." That is a preemptive tactic that exposes the unwillingness of GWA to consider whether global warming is actually happening or the extent to which humans may be responsible. GWA also try to stifle anyone who suggests that mankind might not be the primary cause of global warming.

GWA often blather that a "consensus of scientists" agrees that the Earth is warming and that it is being caused by man. However, consensus is irrelevant in science. An hypothesis is either scientifically correct or it isn't. Just because many scientists agree that man is causing global warming doesn't mean they are scientifically correct. A consensus of scientists in Galileo's time thought the Sun revolved around the Earth.

GWA have used the appeal to authority argument to support their positions on global warming. As noted above, consensus does not equate to scientific fact and that is true on both sides of the global warming controversy. Nonetheless, we skeptics can also play the authority game (11). There are numerous climate experts (Richard Lindzen, Roy Spencer, S. Fred Singer, Howard Hayden, Joe Bastardi, Patrick Michaels, Henrik Svensmark, William Gray, Robert Balling, Jr. and Robert Carter, to name just a few) who do not accept that humans are the chief cause of global warming. Unlike Al Gore and Leonardo DiCaprio, these are true scientists and are knowledgeable in the intricacies of climate. Hayden wrote an excellent rebuttal to GWA contentions; his letter to Lisa Jackson, then Administrator of the EPA, is reproduced in the chapter notes (12).

Though I'm only a humble chemist, I've been called a CCD (climate change denier). Quite the contrary, I have never denied that the

Earth may be warming. Perhaps the world is indeed warming; it has in the past and it will in the future. However, it is not possible to judge whether warming is truly happening based on 10 decades of data. Climate has been changing for more than 4 billion years and 100 years amount to less than 0.000003% of the age of the Earth. (Interestingly, some experts have even suggested that the Earth has been *cooling* since the unusually warm El Niño year of 1998.) It is a certainty that the Earth will get warmer (and cooler) in the coming epochs. Many climate scientists concede that humankind may be responsible for a *minor* portion of warming. However, the human contribution is likely so small that it gets lost in the baseline noise. At this point, it definitely does not warrant Americans to revert to living standards from the 1800s. Neither should Americans be required to pay exorbitant electric bills because antihumanists insist that government mandate that a portion of electric energy come from windmills or solar panels.

Climate has never been static. It will forever be dynamic. Global warming is a perfectly natural occurrence about which humankind can do little. Cap-and-trade schemes and carbon taxes may enrich the US Treasury, but will not stop global warming. For me, that is the crux of the matter. Too many antihumanists want government to impose drastic, expensive actions that will have little impact on climate.

However, the consequences for poor countries may be huge, considering what activists want to do to stop global warming. Mandating that use of fossil fuels be drastically reduced will impact Third World countries disproportionately and doom their poor to a continued meager existence. It appears that GWA don't want the Third World to have electricity, flush toilets, clean water or automobiles. Where's the compassion of leftists for the poor?

The late Michael Crichton expressed a similar sentiment about the developing world and ideological environmentalism (13). Crichton suggests that the West is essentially telling the developing world: *We got ours and we don't want you to get yours, because you'll cause too much pollution.*

In my experience, arguing with a GWA is pointless and I no longer indulge in such useless exercises. Many have little appreciation of the enormity of the 4,500,000,000 years that the Earth has been in existence and the fact that climate changes have occurred throughout its long history. They are unwilling to consider that humans have walked the Earth for a mere few million years, at most. That amounts to *less than 0.06% of the age of the Earth*. They blithely ignore The Medieval Climate Optimum and The Maunder Minimum, during which the so-called Little Ice Age occurred. Nor do they appreciate that hundreds of millions of years ago, CO2 concentrations in the atmosphere were in the many thousands of ppm without any help from humans. Nevertheless, Earth, and especially plant life, did just fine. Often, GWA simply regurgitate the Al Gore mantra about anthropogenic global warming or resort to *ad hominem* attacks. GWA would never accept my view of climate change and I won't accede to their fallacious arguments. So, what's the use? Arguing with GWA reminds me of a line from a 1970 Ray Stevens song (*Everything is Beautiful*) which says:

There is none so blind, as he who will not see...

GWA stubbornly cling to their beliefs that the greenhouse gas carbon dioxide (CO_2) is the culprit and that mankind is responsible for putting most of the CO_2 in the atmosphere. However, Hayden has estimated that mankind is responsible for less than 5% of atmospheric CO_2 (14). Also, paleo records indicate that much higher levels of CO_2 were present in the atmosphere long before humankind and ICE existed (15). Furthermore, the contribution of water, the most important greenhouse gas, may be downplayed or misjudged. In temperate and tropical climates, water is typically present in the atmosphere in quantities much greater than CO_2 (16).

Is Carbon Dioxide Evil?

In Chapter 4, I mentioned a misinformed blogger who suggested that carbon is evil. That must mean that carbon dioxide is also evil. GWA apparently think so. Since GWA insist that atmospheric CO_2 is the most important cause of global warming, let's take a closer look at carbon dioxide. Let's start with a few points about which we skeptics and GWA are in agreement. We agree that CO_2 is a greenhouse gas which causes heat to be trapped in Earth's atmosphere (and it's a good thing, because without greenhouse gases, Earth would be too cold and we wouldn't be here). It is also not disputed that CO_2 in the atmosphere has increased from about 0.028% (280 ppm) just prior to the Industrial Revolution to today's level of about 0.039% (390 ppm) over the past couple of centuries. However, as mentioned above, CO_2 was present in the atmosphere in concentrations of *thousands* of ppm in the distant geologic past. That was a perfectly natural phenomenon. The plants loved it and grew in profusion in what is now called the Jurassic period, (roughly 150-200 million years ago, approximately at the beginning of the age of the dinosaurs).

Key points of *disagreement* between skeptics and GWA are the following:

- ▸ mankind has caused global warming,
- ▸ emissions of CO_2 by mankind is the primary cause, and
- ▸ urgent measures must be taken to stop global warming.

Paleo records show that about 500 million years ago, CO_2 levels were roughly 15-20 times higher than the so-called pre-industrial level of 280 ppm, or about 4000-6000 ppm (15). The concentration then decreased to about 400 ppm over about the next 200 million years. The concentration then increased to another peak of about 1000 ppm 100 million years ago. CO_2 concentration then gradually decreased to the levels we see today. However, as noted above, modern measurements over the past couple of centuries have shown that atmospheric CO_2 has increased to ~390 ppm, approximately the same as it was 300 million years ago.

CO_2 is a combustion product of fossil fuels. It is an odorless, colorless gas. It is produced when we burn gasoline in our vehicles and when coal and natural gas are burned in our power plants to generate electricity. It is also the gas that we exhale during respiration and the dissolved gas that gives soft drinks their fizz. CO_2 occurs widely in nature; for example, it is a major component in the gases liberated by volcanoes. We commonly encounter low CO_2 concentrations in everyday life without adverse effects. However, it is true that CO_2 may become an acute systemic toxin at *elevated* concentrations. That is, it is not a simple asphyxiant. The permissible exposure limit (PEL) set by OSHA for CO_2 is 5000 ppm, suggesting a relatively low order of toxicity. (PEL is the highest time-weighted average concentration to which a worker can be safely exposed in an 8-hour workday.)

Carbon dioxide should not be confused with carbon monoxide (CO) which is much more toxic than CO_2. The OSHA PEL for CO is 50 ppm, indicating much greater toxicity than CO_2. Carbon monoxide can result from incomplete combustion of fossil fuels such as natural gas. CO has been responsible for occasional poisoning deaths in the home because of faulty heating systems. CO is present in very low concentrations ($\sim$0.2 ppm) in air.

One of the most preposterous rulings in the history of the US Supreme Court was their declaration in 2007 that CO_2 is a pollutant and subject to regulation by the EPA. This ruling by the "Supremes" was even more wrongheaded than their ruling on Obamacare. (See Chapter 9.) GWA and environmental activists lauded this misguided ruling. How ridiculous is it that the gas that you exhale when breathing is declared a pollutant?! What happened to common sense? Now GWA can (and will) push the EPA to regulate CO_2 emissions from power plants, automobiles, back yard grills, lawnmowers, airplanes and a host other potential sources of CO_2. American citizens will pay the price.

Because CO_2 levels are at the heart of the GWA contention that mankind is causing global warming, permit me to reiterate several key points. It is indisputable that CO_2 has increased in the atmosphere since the beginning of the industrial revolution. It is also agreed that CO_2 is a greenhouse gas and that mankind may be responsible for a *portion* of climate change. *What is disputed* is the GWA claim that mankind is the *primary* cause of global warming because burning of fossil fuels puts too much CO_2 in the atmosphere. This, despite estimates that indicate man is responsible for less than 5% of the CO_2 that enters the atmosphere annually (14). The carbon cycle is very complex and is not completely understood. Natural sources of CO_2 in the atmosphere (soil respiration and release from warm oceans) dwarf human causes (17).

GWA often cite mankind's response to the depletion of stratospheric ozone (see Montreal Protocol) as a model for what should be done now to stop global warming. But there are large differences between the two circumstances and the two are not truly comparable. The chemistry of ozone depletion in the stratosphere could be simulated and tested under controlled conditions in the laboratory. Paul Crutzen, Frank Rowland and Mario Molina were awarded the 1995 Nobel Prize (18) in chemistry for their work on ozone depletion. Chlorofluorocarbons (CFCs), used as coolants in air-conditioning systems among other large-scale applications, were thought to be particularly damaging via mechanisms involving chlorine atoms and free radicals. Free radical chemistry is widely used in organic chemistry, is relatively well-understood and has been employed industrially since the late 1930s to produce low density polyethylene, poly(vinyl chloride) and many other polymers (19).

In contrast to free radical chemistry, global weather is an enormously complex, chaotic system. Global warming is not well understood and cannot be simulated in laboratories. Consequently, climate scientists rely on computer models. Computer-generated "general circulation models" (GCM) for climate are being used extensively. But, because climate scientists are attempting to model a complex phenomenon with many variables that are not well understood, the models are presently of limited value. The old maxim of "garbage in, garbage out" for computer applications clearly applies to some of today's computer simulations for climate change. Huber expressed his view on computer models in his book *Hard Green* as follows (20):

The computers can multiply the invisible by the infinite to arrive at any number they please. The models can link any human activity, however small, to any environmental consequence, however large...To the Soft Green, the model is everything... Only the model can explain whether our backyard barbecues (collectively, of course) are going to alter the rainfall in Rwanda...

The intricacies of carbon sources and sinks are beyond the scope of this book, but Hayden wrote an excellent overview of key aspects (17). Water is the most important greenhouse gas (22), but the hydrologic cycle is also not well understood and the impact of water on climate is sometimes downplayed or completely ignored in the models. The late Michael Crichton offered the following comment on models (23):

Nobody knows how much warming will occur in the next century. The computer models vary by 400 percent, de facto proof that nobody knows....

Before leaving the subject of CO_2, we should consider a couple of techniques called geoengineering that have been suggested to mitigate carbon dioxide in the atmosphere. These approaches involve using technology to modify the climate (24).

The first is called carbon sequestration. As previously mentioned, carbon dioxide and water are generated when fossil fuels are combusted. Sequestration involves capture of CO_2 and disposal, typically by deep well injection. CO_2 and water from power plants have historically been released into the atmosphere, which is objectionable to GWA. Since the Supreme Court made its ridiculous ruling that CO_2 may be regulated as a pollutant, Mr. Obama's EPA may soon require utilities to lower CO_2 emissions. As we saw in Chapter 4, this will add enormous costs and will put some plants out of business, especially older coal-burning plants. Are you ready for brownouts?! Just as Obama predicted, Americans will see their electricity bills skyrocket. Requiring carbon capture and sequestration is a perfect illustration of the harm that can result by trying to stop global warming.

The second geoengineering technique suggested for CO_2 mitigation is to introduce iron to oceans to promote growth of phytoplankton, which absorbs CO_2. An unauthorized dumping of iron-laden dust off the coast of British Columbia was reported in October of 2012. A satellite map of chlorophyll concentration showed a plankton bloom in the area (24).

Geoengineering to stop climate change is another boondoggle. It will be expensive, and unnecessary, not to mention possible unintended consequences that might occur. Unfortunately, I fear that activists will succeed in goading governments to implement geoengineering schemes.

Cosmologists tell us that the sun will begin its death throes in about 5 billion years by becoming a red giant and it will engulf the inner planets, possibly including Earth. There's nothing mankind can do to stop the red giant phase, even if humans are still around in that distant future. Should the UN form an "IPCCS" (Intergovernmental Panel on Climate Changes on the Sun)? Absurd, I know, but trying to stop climate change on Earth may be only slightly less ludicrous. It is the height of hubris for humans to think that mankind can control climate with today's meager understanding of the complexities of weather. (For the worrywarts among us, 5 billion years is virtually "forever" on the human time scale. Don't worry, be happy.)

The Precautionary Principle

The so-called Precautionary Principle is often invoked as a bromide that should be applied to the global warming problem. The principle originated in Germany where it was called *Vorsorgeprinzip*. It is a benign-sounding concept suggesting that steps should be taken "just in case" the GWA are correct, but implies that actions to stop global warming have little or no consequences. The reality is that such measures will have drastic consequences. According to the principle, measures should be taken, even if scientific proof of harm is lacking. The principle, which came to prominence at the UN environmental conference in Rio de Janiero in 1992, may be concisely stated as follows: "Where there are threats of serious or irreversible damage, lack of full scientific certainty shall not be used as a reason for postponing cost-effective measures to prevent environmental degradation" (25).

The Precautionary Principle has been discredited by many who do not accept that mankind has caused (and is causing) climate change. The following perspectives were offered by the late Michael Crichton (26):

- ► *I conclude that most environmental "principles" (such as sustainable development or the precautionary principle) have the effect of preserving the economic advantages of the West and thus constitute modern imperialism toward the developing world. It is a nice way of saying, "We got ours and we don't want you to get yours, because you'll cause too much pollution."*
- ► *The "precautionary principle," properly applied, forbids the precautionary principle. It is self-contradictory. The precautionary principle therefore cannot be spoken of in terms that are too harsh.*

The Precautionary Principle has also been described as a moral precept masquerading under a scientific cloak (27). Adler concluded his discussion of the Precautionary Principle with the following remark (28): *The precautionary principle's threat to technological progress is itself a threat to public health and environmental protection. The world would be safer without it.*

Advocates of the precautionary principle are risk-averse Neo-Luddites, opposed to new technology simply because it's new. Rather than using some arbitrary principle, new technology should be evaluated based upon a thorough assessment of the risks and benefits to humankind and the environment.

Conclusion

It should be evident that America (and indeed the entire world) is being harmed by the global warming boondoggle. It has already cost billions and will cost even more in the not-too-distant future as GWA, antihumanists and watermelons continue their assault on the modern way of life. What's worse is that it is a gigantic waste of taxpayer money. It will degrade living standards and cause everything to cost much more, from your groceries, to the electricity for your home, to the clothes you wear. It will disproportionately hurt the poor and doom the Third World to continued subsistence living. All for something that is going to happen no matter what governments do.

The fossil fuel industries have been especially targeted by environmentalist loons who want America to "return to nature" to stop global warming. Oil, coal and natural gas industries are regularly demonized, though these natural resources are absolutely essential for modern life. Coal has been especially targeted by activists who have seen to it that burdensome regulations have been imposed in an attempt to drive coal companies out of business.

As I was putting the finishing touches on this chapter, I came across an article on the Internet. It was about the so-called Doomsday Clock for 2013 being kept at 5 minutes to midnight and appeared in the *Bulletin of Atomic Scientists* (29). It was mentioned in an open letter to President Obama. The first sentence of their section on climate reveals that their starting point is the fallacious GWA mantra: *Human activities are now the <u>dominant</u> cause of global climate change* (my emphasis). Of course, as we have suggested in this chapter, warming may indeed be happening, but mankind is not the dominant cause.

Among my greatest concerns are the regulations and laws that the legislature and Obama's agencies (most notably the EPA) will impose in the name of stopping global warming. This amounts to nothing more than squandering US treasure. Moreover, as Hayden has suggested (14), humans are responsible for a very small percentage of CO_2 that enters the atmosphere. Capture and sequestration of CO_2 from the flue gases of power plants will be hugely expensive. If government mandates sequestration of CO_2, costs of American electricity will indeed skyrocket, just as Mr. Obama predicted. That is true, even if all power plants convert to less costly natural gas as fuel. Unfortunately, CO_2 sequestration appears to be the path that Mr. Obama and comrades want to follow.

A recent issue of *Chemical & Engineering News*, the weekly trade magazine of the American Chemical Society of which I have been a member for many years, contained no less than three articles having to do with some aspect of climate change (30). The articles addressed cap-and-trade schemes, carbon taxes and measures that Europe and California are taking to force reductions in CO_2 emissions. To borrow a Shakespearean phrase, this is "Much Ado about Nothing." Unfortunately, such actions appear to be inevitable, but will be a colossal waste of money.

I close this chapter with a statement made by Paul Johnston in a preface in Robert Carter's book entitled *Climate: The Counter Consensus"* (31):

> *The idea that human beings have changed and are changing the basic climate system of the Earth through their industrial activities and burning of fossil fuels—the essence of the Greens' theory of global warming—has about as much basis in science as Marxism and Freudianism. Global warming, like Marxism, is a political theory of actions, demanding compliance with its rules. Marxism, Freudianism, global warming. These are proof –of which history offers so many examples—that people can be suckers on a grand scale. To their fanatical followers they are a substitute for religion. Global warming, in particular, is a creed, a faith, a dogma that has little to do with science....*

Chapter 7

VOTING AND INCOME TAXES

The hardest thing in the world to understand is the income tax.

Albert Einstein

Who Should Be Allowed to Vote?

VOTING IS THE VERY FOUNDATION of a democracy. Properly administered, voting amounts to a chance for ordinary citizens to have a say in how government spends their tax money. However, great harm has been inflicted on America by voter fraud. In close elections, these fraudulent votes sometimes change the direction of the country. The shenanigans of Chicago Mayor Richard Daley in Illinois that helped elect John Kennedy in 1960 have become political lore. A more recent example was the narrow election of former *Saturday Night Live* comedian Al Franken as senator in Minnesota by what were clearly fraudulent votes (1). How many fraudulent votes were cast? We'll never know, but it is clear that many more were for Franken. Because Franken was narrowly "elected," his vote eventually became the one that allowed the abomination known as Obamacare to pass the senate. The joke's on the American people.

Another anecdote about voter fraud recently came to light. A Cincinnati woman openly admitted that she cast *at least* two votes for President Obama in the 2012 election (2). How many others voted multiple times?

No discussion of voter fraud would be complete without, at least, a mention of the defunct Association of Community Organizations for Reform Now, better known as ACORN. This organization committed voter fraud on a massive scale (3). ACORN was truly adept at registering the cemetery vote mentioned in Chapter 3. ACORN was ultimately defunded by Congress and filed Chapter 7 bankruptcy in 2010. Though ACORN no longer exists, there are spinoffs with new names. In effect, the organization was simply rebranded.

Despite examples of fraud, liberals remain vehemently opposed to requiring citizens to show a picture ID before being allowed to vote. What's so onerous about that? A picture ID is required for so many commonplace transactions, *e.g.*, cashing a check and obtaining a driver's license. But Democrats claim that requiring photo ID is discriminatory. They don't wish to prohibit illegal aliens, felons or the deceased from voting. They are important parts of their base.

Recently, I listened to Michael Berry, a popular radio talk show host in the Houston area. Berry contended that 18-yr olds should not be allowed to vote and suggested that the minimum age for voting should be 25. He apparently believes that most 18-yr olds do not have the maturity that comes with a range of life experiences. I surmise he thinks they are not sufficiently aware of the ways of the world and are incapable of discerning which candidate would govern more wisely.

Many young voters simply don't care about politics and haven't been paying attention. They often have a frivolous, superficial view of elections. Most are much more concerned with the opposite sex, the latest music videos, or the newest electronic gadgets, than with the candidates' positions on energy or the national debt. Not all young voters are stupid, though they may be ignorant. (Ignorance can be corrected, but stupid is forever.) The crux of the matter is this: the vote of a young ignoramus may cancel the vote of an informed, responsible citizen. Ignorant votes count precisely the same as informed votes.

I realize that changing the voting age to exclude young voters will be considered as soon as Democrats seek lower taxes. A compelling argument in favor of the 18-yr old vote is: if they can be drafted into the armed services to fight (and possibly die) for their country, they should be able to vote. That's a strong case for the 18-year old vote. Rather than changing the voting age, I think it would be better to require all voters to demonstrate that they have at least an elementary understanding of civics, American history and the US democratic process.

It's a near certainty that I share few views with liberal CNN columnist LZ Granderson on political matters. Nonetheless, we are both in favor of preventing the ignorant from voting (4). On the other side of the issue, Frank Hagler called preventing the ignorant from voting a form of "political snobbery" (5). Further, Hagler suggested that there was no "fair and equitable way to ensure that voters are well-informed and 'up-to-speed' on the issues." He implied that such a system would be unworkable.

Well, call me a political snob, but I think it is folly to allow the oblivious to have a say in the direction of the country. While it would be good to insure that voters are up-to-speed on current events, that is less important than insuring that they know sixth grade level facts about government and US history. Hagler is mistaken. In the age of computers, it would be quite easy to put a system in place using multiple choice questions.

A voter need not be a member of Mensa to qualify. However, voters should know the answers to simple questions about US government and history. A voter could be asked 8 or 10 very simple multiple choice questions before the computer would provide a ballot. This would minimize the contributions of moron voters discussed in Chapter 3. At the considerable risk of insulting your intelligence, I provide a few examples below:

- ► What are the three branches of the US government?
    - a) Defense, commerce and education
    - b) Environment, labor, and health and human services
    - c) Senate, House of Representatives, Department of State
    - d) Legislative, executive and judicial

- ► How many senators are elected from each state?
    - a) 2
    - b) 3
    - c) 4
    - d) Depends on population of state

- ► Which political party favors strong defense, lower taxes, and limited government?
    - a) Republican
    - b) Democrat
    - c) Socialist

d) Communist

- How many states currently make up the USA?
    - a) 57
    - b) 51
    - c) 50
    - d) 48

- In what years did the US fight in The Second World War?
    - a) 1914-1918
    - b) 1941-1945
    - c) 1950-1953
    - d) 1965-1973

- What do North Korea, China and Cuba have in common?
    - a) They are all communist states
    - b) They all have nuclear weapons
    - c) They are all on the Asian continent.
    - d) They are all major producers of oil

- Who became president when Franklin Roosevelt died in 1945?
    - a) Gerald Ford
    - b) Calvin Coolidge
    - c) Cosmo Kramer
    - d) Harry Truman

- How many justices sit on the Supreme Court?
    - a) 3
    - b) 6
    - c) 9
    - d) 12

- Which president was responsible for *The Great Society* program?

a) Barack Obama
b) Lyndon Johnson
c) Bill Clinton
d) Dwight Eisenhower

▸ Which president was responsible for *The New Deal*?
a) George Harrison
b) Franklin Roosevelt
c) Theodore Roosevelt
d) Ronald Reagan

▸ How many Representatives are elected from each state?
a) 2
b) 3
c) 4
d) Depends on population of state

▸ Which president was responsible for establishing the EPA and OSHA?
a) Jimmy Carter
b) Woodrow Wilson
c) John Kennedy
d) Richard Nixon

▸ Which of the following were among the Axis countries opposing the US in World War II?
a) Germany, Iraq and Spain
b) Japan, France and Russia
c) China, Italy and Iran
d) Italy, Japan and Germany

If a prospective voter answers 50% or more of the questions correctly he/she could be deemed qualified to vote. If a voter gets less than 50% correct, he or she should not receive a ballot and should be disqualified from voting in that election. A voter who can't get at least half of these ridiculously easy questions correct, is clearly ignorant and has no business voting. Both of my 11-year old granddaughters in the 6th grade easily passed the test. Given that the questions are only slightly more difficult than Groucho Marx's famous question (Who is buried in Grant's tomb?*), this seems eminently fair and might keep the oblivious from electing another nincompoop like Al Franken. Did you get more than 50% correct? (Answers in Appendix).

It is sad commentary on the state of education in America to note that many 18-year olds (and more than a few adults) would fail this test. The teeny bopper who knows well the latest trends in popular music or electronic games might not be able to vote. However, that will be no loss since his or her vote might cancel the vote of a truly informed citizen. Yes, ignorant persons will be disenfranchised and liberals will howl. And yes, it's discriminatory, because it would prevent the clueless from voting. However, the ignorant will not be allowed to influence the direction of the country. As previously suggested, I realize that such a system has as much a chance as a snowball in hell. The Thought Police would never allow it. They will complain that it is unfair.

Income Taxes and Fair Share

It is not only the ignorant who should be prohibited from voting. Another group that should not be allowed to vote are the nearly half of US wage-earners who pay zero in income taxes. With the present tax structure, what incentive do they have to demand that government control spending? Why would they care if President Obama raises taxes on the so-called rich, as long as they continue to pay zero? Is it fair for them to pay nothing and to be able to cast votes to insure

* Groucho used the question on his 1950s TV show, You Bet Your Life. Though the correct answer was "no one," Groucho accepted Grant so that the person would win a consolation prize.

that their fellow citizens continue to carry the entire income tax burden? I don't think so. They have "no skin in the game," to use President Obama's own words. Yes, this is also discriminatory, but those exempt from paying income taxes (other than the poor) should not be allowed to influence how taxes are spent.

Income taxes typically comprise just over 40% of government revenue. I now agree with President Obama that they're not fair. Mr. Obama has never addressed what a fair share is for those who pay nothing, though he has endlessly ranted that the so-called rich should pay more "a little more" in the name of fairness, a subject discussed further below. However, if you are not poor and you pay no income taxes, you should not be allowed to vote. The slogan used in the original Boston Tea Party needs to be juxtaposed to convey a different concept: NO REPRESENTATION WITHOUT TAXATION!

Most citizens don't fully realize how much they are paying because the government uses the trick of the pay-as-you-go installment plan (withholding). Government takes a portion of each paycheck over the entire year such that taxpayers are less likely to notice how much of their pay is confiscated by government. Those who overpay (and thereby allow Uncle Sam to use their money interest-free for a year) get a refund and some think how magnanimous the Feds are for returning a portion of their money. These taxpayers use withholding as a forced savings plan, which pays zero interest. If the government were to stop withholding and citizens had to write a check to the IRS every April, there would be greater awareness of the true burden of income taxes. However, that that will happen shortly after global warming causes it to snow in Honolulu.

Conservatives usually oppose higher taxes and, in most circumstances, I agree with that principle. While it is true that a modicum of taxes must be collected to take care of the national defense, infrastructure and essential services (including providing for the truly poor and less fortunate), I favor limiting the size of government because smaller government costs less, is less bureaucratic, is more efficient and is less intrusive into personal freedoms of its citizens. Also, lower taxes encourage businesses to invest and expand operations which lead to more jobs and a vibrant economy. It has been shown on several occasions that lowering tax rates actually INCREASES revenues to the Treasury because businesses pay more taxes from expanded sales. During my lifetime, that was irrefutably demonstrated by Democrat John F. Kennedy, and Republicans Ronald Reagan and George W. Bush. Each reduced tax rates leading to an improved economy and increased tax dollars going to the US treasury. Why can't today's Democrats grasp this simple fact?

Let's take a closer look at President Obama's viewpoint on income tax. He believes that the rich are not paying their fair share of income taxes. The rich is a moving target, depending who in the Obama administration is speaking. In 2011, Obama proposed the "Buffet Rule" to tax millionaires. The fabulously wealthy Warren Buffet famously claimed that his secretary paid more income taxes (as a percentage of income) than he. The Buffet Rule was proposed to insure that the rich pay more, such that a millionaire would never pay less than a humble secretary. However, the Buffet rule is nothing more than a red herring. It is a means of punishing success or achievement. It is disgusting to hear Mr. Obama and his sycophants whine about the rich not paying their fair share of income taxes, when the top 10% of wage-earners already pay over 70% of the income taxes! How fair is it that nearly half of the wage earners in the US pay no income tax at all?

Democrats have an aversion for the word "taxes." It's part of their war on language (discussed in Chapter 8). They try just about anything to avoid using it. It's been that way since at least the Bill Clinton days. The Clintonistas used to talk about investing in the future of children. That was Clinton code for: *We want more of your money and we're going to increase your taxes.* More recently, liberals talk about increasing revenues and forcing the rich to pay their fair share. No amount of taxes will ever be enough for leftists. It appears that they want to confiscate everything you make so they can redistribute it. There's a name for that—it's called socialism (or communism).

I can hear the bleeding heart liberals trashing me because they jumped to the conclusion that I suggest that the poor be taxed. Perish the thought! No doubt, liberals will complain that the poor are taxed alternatively, by sales and payroll taxes, for example. While it is true that poverty can never be completely eliminated, I agree fully that the poor should pay no income tax and that government should provide a safety net. _However, there is no way that nearly half of the American population is in poverty._ In 2010, the Census Bureau determined that about 15% of Americans were in poverty, using the government's definition of poverty. Actually, the percentage of Americans living in poverty, as defined by government, has changed little since the administration of Lyndon B. Johnson in the late 1960s, hovering between 11 and 15% (6).

In the 1960s, LBJ launched the so-called _War on Poverty_. It was a colossal failure that cost _trillions_ with little impact on poverty. I remember well a clever line from the 1970s song _Nothing from Nothing_ by the late Billy Preston, in which he proclaimed that he was a "soldier in the War on Poverty." However, Preston and his fellow soldiers apparently lost the war. Estimates indicate that the US has spent about $16.7 trillion on the War on Poverty, almost matching the national debt in 2013 (7). There should be a bracket where the poor are exempt from paying income tax. Beyond that, everyone should pay something, even if it's only 2%. Will we ever hear President Obama suggest something like that? Perhaps when Bill Maher praises Sarah Palin.

America shouldn't continue with nearly half its wage-earners paying nothing in income tax. As Obama and his ilk are wont to say: it isn't fair. A complete overhaul of the tax code is needed. As suggested above, all voting citizens except those in poverty should pay something. Free riders could be reduced to about 15%, the poverty rate calculated using government guidelines from the 2010 census. The existing progressive scale could be retained, which should delight Democrats, because it places most of the income tax burden on high wage earners. However, because there would be an increase in the percentage of wage earners paying tax from the present ~52% to ~85%, revenues to the Treasury would increase.

Imagine for a moment that President Obama has imposed an income tax on wage-earners who are currently paying zero. Additional taxes shouldn't be too difficult to envision for him, since Mr. Obama has never seen a tax that he would oppose, especially if it is in the interest of so-called fairness. Since revenues to the Treasury would increase, do you think President Obama might lower the rate on other taxpayers in some equitable way? Not a chance! The best America could hope for is that he would apply the surplus to reduce the national debt.

Chapter 8

POLITICAL CORRECTNESS
AND HIGHER EDUCATION

America will never be destroyed from the outside. If we falter and lose our freedoms, it will be because we destroyed ourselves.

Abraham Lincoln

Introduction

AMERICA HAS BECOME A COUNTRY obsessed with political correctness. Almost all of what is considered politically correct has been proffered by leftists trying to change what they consider to be inappropriate or insensitive behavior by people they think to be less attuned to the sensibilities of others. It has become almost clichéd to use PC speech.

George Orwell's classic novel (*1984*) about the evils of totalitarianism was published in 1949 (1). It was his cynical view of a future in which government controlled every aspect of life, including their attempt to control citizens' very thoughts. He wrote about *Newspeak*, the official language of the fictional Oceania where Winston Smith (the protagonist) lived.

Orwellian Newspeak and today's politically correct speech have at least one feature in common. Both attempt to substitute alternative wording for what proponents consider unacceptable (or unnecessary) speech. In *1984*, Big Brother used Newspeak as a means of mind-control and wanted Newspeak to replace what was called the *Old Language*.

As suggested above, politically correct speech may be considered an attempt to control thought. To my knowledge, there are now no federal laws in America that mandate politically correct *speech*. Is it possible that political correctness might lead to regulations and infringe upon individual liberties? It already has in certain liberal strongholds. For example, New York City's Mayor Michael Bloomberg, the self-appointed health policeman for the Nanny state, has banned *trans* fat in NYC restaurants and is currently trying to block sale of large, sugary soft drinks.

Are leftists attempting to incite further class warfare using political correctness, just as they have with the rich-poor dissension, the red-blue states division and the Haves-Have Nots conflict discussed by

Saul Alinsky (2)? (Recall the phony Democrat charge that Republicans were waging a *war on women.*) Dividing an already highly fragmented society into additional subgroups can only lead to even greater polarization of the country.

The poor quality of education in America was mentioned in passing in Chapter 7. Among the more serious problems is the leftist slant in academia. While universities usually strive to achieve diversity in student demographics, teachers with conservative views are *persona non grata* and woefully underrepresented on their faculties. Faculty recruiting committees might as well put up a sign saying "Conservatives need not apply." What happened to the left's abhorrence for anything discriminatory and desire for diversity? According to David Horowitz, the faculty at The University of Colorado is about 30:1 liberals to conservatives (3). How many conservative professors are on the faculty at Harvard? Not many, I'm sure.

Political correctness and the leftward slant in academia enable liberal professors to inculcate students with progressive thought. True, some effects may be considered frivolous and inconsequential, but others are serious intrusions on individual freedoms. The damage to America will continue to be felt in local and national elections with the continued slide to the left, resulting in unnecessary laws and regulations attempting to control every aspect of existence.

Before addressing indoctrination in the educational system and political correctness, I should mention that *ideally* neither liberal nor conservative viewpoints should be promoted in the classroom. Teachers should present facts, without favoring one philosophy over another. Students should draw their own conclusions. However, with the composition of university faculties, that is rarely the case.

Leftists in Academia

Unfortunately, it is not uncommon for liberal professors to proselytize in the classroom, attempting to indoctrinate students in their leftist worldview. Students are instructed on the fine points of Alinskyism, political correctness and contempt for anything conservative. Though Alinsky urged non-violence, some liberal professors openly advocate violence. In many cases, university political science departments have been transformed into western versions of madrassas for the training of future generations of America-hating leftists. Horowitz, a self-described former Marxist (4), wrote a book about professors he considered to be the most flagrant examples of leftist bias in American colleges and universities. Horowitz used an obscure selection method called "prosopography." Horowitz concluded the introduction to his book with the following statement:

> *My most difficult task in writing this book was living daily with the knowledge it provides of the enormous damage that several generations of tenured radicals have inflicted on our educational system; and being cognizant of the unrelenting malice that so many of them hold in their hearts for a country that has given them the great privileges and freedoms they enjoy as a birthright.*

The professors on his list (5) harbor an eclectic mix of extreme left-wing philosophies. Horowitz provided a short profile for each professor. Sprinkled throughout those profiles were descriptors like anti-white, communist, anti-American, anti-Semitic, Maoist, Marxist, Marxist-feminist and Leninist. These radical philosophies are being taught to young American students. Horowitz opined that *the professorial task is to teach students, not to tell them what to think.* Unfortunately, too many ignore that principle (7). Several of the Professors selected by Horowitz are aging radicals frozen in the 1960s.

Of course, Horowitz could only list those he believed to be the most egregious examples of ideological professors. He estimated there are 25,000 to 30,000 leftist professors in US colleges and that they teach about 3 million students each school year (7). The radical positions espoused by these professors may be illustrated by

Horowitz's profiles of Professors Jose Angel Gutierrez and Nicholas De Genova.

Professor Gutierrez threatened gringoes with the following statement: *We have got to eliminate the gringo, and what I mean by that is if worst comes to worst, we have got to kill him.* Professor De Genova expressed the hope that America would experience "a million Mogadishus" in its 2003 war with Iraq. (De Genova was alluding to the ill-fated military operation in Mogadishu, Somalia in October of 1993 during which 18 US soldiers were killed. The episode was immortalized in the book and movie *Black Hawk Down.*)

Figure 8.1 shows the geographic distributions of the radical professors listed by Horowitz. Though non-scientific, it is enlightening to note that more than half of Horowitz's professors are from schools in the northeast part of America, probably the bluest region of the continental US and a stronghold of the Democrat Party.

Figure 8.1 Locations of "Radical" Professors in the US

(Compiled from Horowitz's list [5])

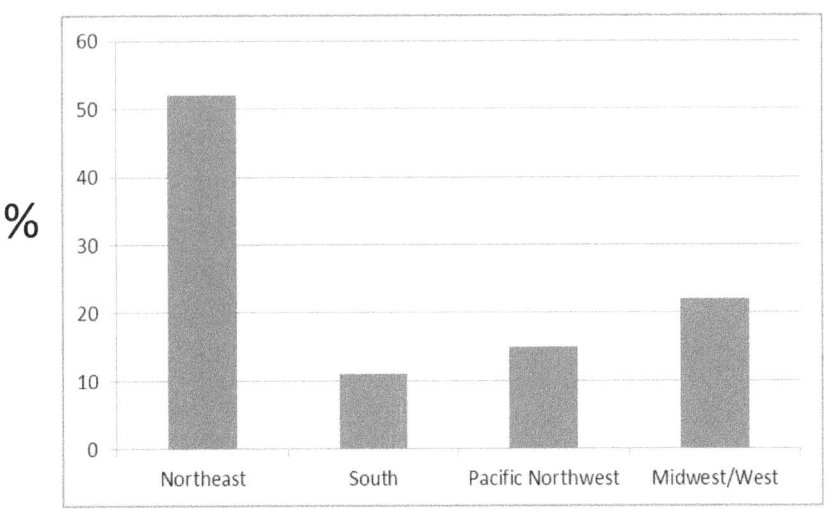

In effect, professors identified by Horowitz and thousands of like-minded comrades across academia in America constitute a fifth column intent upon undermining America. Is it any wonder that America is in decline?

Political Correctness

Political correctness is largely a phenomenon of the left. PC speech has become commonplace in today's vernacular. Political correctness is intended to shield members of protected groups from what liberals perceive to be hurtful or discriminatory speech. To be considered politically correct, one must avoid figures of speech or phraseology that could be interpreted as an affront based on gender, race, a handicap, physical characteristics, etc. I have employed what may be regarded as politically correct terms several times in this book. However, politically correct speech is sometimes carried to ridiculous extremes. It could be considered a war on language, in effect censoring what is deemed acceptable forms of expression. As noted above, PC speech may be considered a type of Orwellian thought control and leftists as the Thought Police. Though leftists are not yet able to arrest citizens for thoughtcrimes as in 1984, they try to shame the politically incorrect and portray them as oblivious, insensitive boors. Though I agree that no one should be insensitive to the feelings of others and offensive names have no place in civil society, I object to the absurd lengths required to be considered politically correct by self-righteous liberals. A few examples of historic usages and the preferred PC term are given below:

Common Usage	_Politically Correct Term_
bald	follicly challenged
black (Negro, colored, etc.)	African-American
blind	visually impaired
chairman	chairperson
deaf	hearing impaired
fireman	firefighter
illegal aliens	undocumented workers
mankind	humankind

policeman	law enforcement officer
retarded	mentally challenged
secretary	administrative assistant
stewardess	flight attendant

You get the drift. These examples only scratch the surface.

When a Senator long venerated by Democrats and a leftist professor used the politically incorrect terms "white nigger" and "gringoes," the silence from much of the self-appointed Thought Police was deafening. Apparently, only conservatives may be accused of political incorrectness or racism.

I know well that there are those who purposely use hateful speech (8), as aforementioned Prof. Gutierrez did when he said that gringoes must be killed. However, being expected to call a bald man follicly challenged seems to be PC carried to absurdity.

Obamunists are fluent in PC speech. It appears that President Obama is determined to use alternative terminology in place of that used during the George Bush era. That's how the war on terror became the "overseas contingency operation." Carol Platt Liebau offered the following observations on the Obama administration's assault on language (9):

> Take, as an example, the host of euphemisms that's been trotted out as part of the Obama Administration's approach to the war on terror. Since 2009, "rogue states" have become "outliers"; vague phrases like "overseas contingency operations," "man-caused disasters," "countering violent extremism" and – most recently – "kinetic military action" have entered the national lexicon.

On November 5, 2009, Major Nidal Hasan entered a building at Fort Hood, TX, shouted *Allahu Akbar!* and opened fire on his Army brothers and sisters, killing 13 and wounding 30. The wounded are now being denied Purple Hearts, in part, because the event was classified as workplace violence rather than the terrorist attack it clearly was. What do Obamunists have against the English language?

In December of 2012, governor of Rhode Island Lincoln Chafee (formerly a RINO as a US Senator, then an independent, and now a Democrat) insisted that the state Christmas tree be called the "Holiday Tree," apparently because he didn't want to offend Muslims, Hindus, Jews, Buddhists, Shintoists, etc. I surmise that he didn't care about offending Christians.

Being politically correct is not restricted to speech. For example, buying a hybrid that gets 40+ mpg or an all electric car makes some feel that they are saving the planet. A survey by Strategic Vision (10) on new car purchases and party affiliation showed that two of the top three choices of Democrats were the Honda Civic Hybrid and the all electric Nissan Leaf. Neither made the top five choices by Republicans. Given the importance of political correctness to the left-leaning, these results are not particularly surprising. It gives liberals the feeling that they are superior to those of us who drive cars with internal combustion engines (11). By driving ICE vehicles, we are "spewing" more CO_2 into the atmosphere thereby contributing to global warming. Note that spewing is the word liberals prefer to describe the liberation of CO_2 into the atmosphere, rather than a less inflammatory word such as "releasing." In an episode of the adult TV cartoon show *South Park*, the writers perfectly satirized sanctimonious owners of hybrids, assigning the name "Pious" (rather than Prius) to their hybrids. I thought it was hilarious, but liberals were probably not amused.

An artificial holiday called Kwanzaa is another example of rampant political correctness. Kwanzaa was invented in the 1960s as a sort of African-American alternative to Christmas. Among other purposes, it was supposed to be a celebration of African cultural heritage. What's next? Celebrating *Festivus* (from a silly *Seinfeld* episode)?

PC terminology has even permeated science abbreviations used for archaeological or geologic periods. For example, the politically correct would say that the Minoan civilization started about 3000 BCE and the Jurassic period was about 200 million years BCE. Use of

BCE, "before the common era," is apparently more politically correct than BC (before Christ). Why? I surmise BCE is deemed less offensive to non-Christian faiths, atheists and agnostics. In place of AD (anno Domini, translated as "in the year of the Lord"), the term common era (or CE) is more politically correct. For example, this is the year 2013 CE, rather than the politically incorrect 2013 AD. Once again, it evidently matters not that Christians may be offended. Should we also rename the months or the days of the week using secular PC names, as the liberal mob did after the French Revolution (13)?

You will sometimes see the politically correct wear small ribbons to signify that they care deeply about the cause of the day. I've done it on occasion for what I consider a worthy cause; perhaps you have also. The cause can range from serious objectives, such as obliterating breast cancer, to the trite, such as saving the snail darter. While eliminating breast cancer would be considered an important, noble and worthwhile endeavor by all reasonable people, the politically *incorrect* will probably regard saving the snail darter an unnecessary exercise. However, if you do not wear a ribbon, you don't care as much as the politically correct (PETA, SPCA, the animal rights people, etc.).

To the extent that political correctness prevents embarrassment and damaged sensibilities, it is harmless, though it may be absurd in some cases. But there are situations where being politically correct can be much more costly to taxpayers.

Is it politically correct to require use of biodegradable or reusable bags for groceries? Recall the case history about the San Francisco Board of Supervisors banning of plastic grocery bags described in Chapter 6. Ban proponents complained that the plastic bags cause unsightly litter on roadways, are not biodegradable, and take up too much room in landfills. Political correctness was an underlying reason for the ban. In effect, the SF Board acted to stop citizens from trashing their beautiful city with non-biodegradable plastics bags without having to call the citizens at fault what they truly are: careless slobs who thoughtlessly litter. The Board also could lay claim to the politically correct goal of "saving the environment" by reducing municipal solid waste going to those dastardly landfills. Such actions are spreading to other PC strongholds in the US, *e.g.*, Austin TX and Seattle WA. Thus far, however, a federal law has not been passed that mandates the entire nation to use reusable canvas bags or bags made from biodegradable plastic (never mind that they cost 2X or 3X more and actually require weeks or months to biodegrade under the ambient conditions of the environment).

At the college national championship football game on January 7, 2013 between Notre Dame and Alabama, an announcer for the game, senior citizen Brent Musberger, commented on a young woman sitting in the stands with the mother of the Alabama quarterback. The young woman was Katherine Webb, a former Miss Alabama USA and the girlfriend of Alabama quarterback, A.J. McCarron. Musberger commented on how beautiful the young woman was. Soon thereafter there was an uproar from the PC crowd about the "inappropriateness" of Musberger's remarks. Among other things, Musberger's comments were called "creepy," "off-putting" and "a personal violation." I don't believe any of the Thought Police called him "a dirty old man," though I'm sure many thought that. Has PC moved the country to the point where a pretty woman cannot be said to be beautiful?

Consider vegetarians and the even more extreme "vegans." I don't know the statistics, but I'm pretty sure a majority of dietary vegans are devout leftists. In principle, dietary vegans avoid foods obtained from animals. Why? Their reasons are probably varied. Perhaps they think that it is healthier to eat foods derived only from plants. Perhaps they are members of SPCA or PETA and believe it is cruel to consume flesh or milk from animals. Perhaps they avoid beef and cow's milk because they believe that cattle contribute to global warming owing to cow flatulence. (Cows are ruminants and emit large quantities of methane from both ends of their digestive systems. Methane is more than 20 times more powerful than carbon dioxide as a greenhouse gas.) Perhaps they do so because they despise "big business." *Whatever their reasons, it's a life-style choice that they have every right to pursue.* I have no problem with them choosing that path. Though I think it's stupid, that's their decision. However, I do not want them requiring that I also become a vegan.

A recent trend has the politically correct crowd calling for changes in the sport of American football. I view this to be part of the left's attempt to prevent any activity that might result in injury, from recess dodge ball in middle schools to college and professional football. Liberal utopians want to remove all risks from life, an impossible dream. The leftist view seems to be that government must protect citizens from their own ignorance. Injuries to the brain from collisions on the football field have come under close scrutiny. Some even question whether the sport should be banned altogether. However, football is a violent, contact sport. Injuries are inevitable. Unless you convert it to "powder puff" or "flag" football, injuries will always be a part of the sport.

In recent years, Nobel Peace Prizes have been awarded more for political correctness than for real accomplishment. Indeed, in some cases, the recipients are laughable. Should Al Gore and the IPCC have been honored for their distortions about anthropogenic global warming? Why was the terrorist Yasser Arafat awarded the Peace Prize? Why should Barack Obama have received the Peace Prize when he was in office for a matter of mere months and had accomplished virtually nothing to promote world peace? Perhaps Mr. Obama received the Nobel Peace Prize for "community organizing." The Nobel Peace Prize has become an international joke.

Politically Correct Mascots

Choices of mascots for university and professional teams may be used to illustrate how thoroughly political correctness has permeated American society. Stanford University had used the "Indians" as its mascot for more than 40 years (14). In 1972, Native American students posited that the name "Indians" was disrespectful. They, along with some faculty, petitioned the Stanford University administration to stop using Indians as the school mascot, claiming that its use was a result of "society's retarded understanding, dulled perception and clouded vision." The university administration ultimately decided that "any and all Stanford University use of the Indian symbol should be immediately disavowed and permanently stopped." And that's how the Stanford Indians became the Stanford Cardinal.

At the University of California-Santa Clara (UCSC), students voted overwhelmingly in 1986 to adopt the name *Banana Slugs* as the school mascot, rather than *Sea Lions* (13). Why did students chose Banana Slugs? One UCSC student explained his reasoning as follows: "*Nobody else is the Banana Slugs, and I don't think any school will ever have a mascot as cool as the slug. It's unique, it's vibrant, it's a little subversive and it represents UC Santa Cruz well.*" A little subversive, I can accept. But I'm not so sure that a phlegmatic slug could be considered vibrant. Perhaps the student is right about the school being represented well by a slimy slug. I was not there to observe the dynamics, but I strongly suspect that a cadre of activist UCSC students influenced their fellow students to vote for the slug. In the tradition of Saul Alinsky, these students wanted Banana Slugs as a means to ridicule the establishment. Leftist students seized the chance to saddle the school with a frivolous, disgusting nickname. Their intentions were likely to embarrass the school administration and to repudiate and denigrate collegiate athletics. They were able to convince a majority of gullible schoolmates, like the young man quoted above, to go along with it to be "cool."

Remarkable because of where it happened, there was what could be considered a "retro" PC change in mascot at The University of Hawaii. Of course, Hawaii is perhaps the bluest of blue states and a bastion of political correctness. Surprisingly, the UH football team opted to change its nickname from the Rainbow Warriors to the Warriors. The name Rainbow was apparently too closely associated with the gay community for many of the athletes and Athletic Director Hugh Yoshida (15). The gay community in the school objected, presumably feeling that the change was insensitive or disrespectful to them. Nevertheless, the change occurred and the university issued an apology to those who might have been offended.

There are yet other university team names that may be considered politically incorrect and may require rebranding. These include the Illinois Fighting Illini, the Florida State Seminoles, the Central Michigan Chippewas, the Notre Dame Fighting Irish, the San Diego State Aztecs, the Utah Utes and the Ole Miss Rebels to name a few. We'll have to see what happens on these.

There is also an ongoing movement today to force some professional sports teams to change their team names to what the Thought Police believe are less offensive names. The professional basketball team formerly known as the Washington Bullets was renamed in 1997 as the Wizards because the violent connotations of bullets, especially in view of the rampant homicides and crime in Washington D.C. (16). In the latter case, it was the team owner who led the effort to change the name. However, this may be just the leading edge of what may be a trend of professional teams changing to names that are considered more politically correct by the Thought Police. The next most likely target is the National Football League team, the Washington Redskins. Soon to follow may be other professional football and baseball teams such as the Cleveland Indians, the Kansas City Chiefs and the Atlanta Braves. The Houston Rockets and Chicago Blackhawks may not be far behind.

Chapter 9

CORRUPTION AND INCOMPETENCE IN GOVERNMENT

Democracy substitutes election by the incompetent many for appointment by the corrupt few.

George Bernard Shaw

Introduction

WRONGDOING AND INCOMPETENCE IN GOVERNMENT have been around since prehistoric cavemen elected their first tribal chief. In recent times, however, it seems that incompetence, corruption, and abuse of power have been uncommonly common in American government. These problems are manifested in all three branches of government, in local governments and in federal agencies, but it is the executive branch that is the greatest concern (1). In true Alinsky fashion, President Obama has bullied, cajoled and obfuscated as he strives to fulfill his vow "to fundamentally transform" America. Regrettably, he has succeeded in far too many ways. Even worse, he's not finished imposing his socialist vision on America.

The American government is out of control. It has grown so large and intrusive as to be unrecognizable relative to the small government envisioned by the founders. Government with limited power that safeguards citizens' right to "life, liberty and the pursuit of happiness" is becoming a thing of the past. Leftists don't really like government to be restricted. Many liberals think the Constitution should be considered a "living document" enabling them to interpret it according to today's standards (or lack thereof). However, the Constitution should not be considered simply a compilation of suggestions or recommendations to be ignored at the whim of leftists. The Constitution should *protect* citizens from intrusive government.

The National Debt

Deficits in America have been a national disgrace for far too long. Washington has a serious spending problem, though President Obama has repeatedly claimed the contrary. It's really quite simple: Washington spends more $ than it has coming in, and it has been doing so for most of the past 50 years. When it needs more, it simply borrows, usually from China, or prints more money. It is a manifestation of incompetence in government. Our grandchildren and great grandchildren will bear the consequences. While both parties must accept some responsibility for overspending, Democrats are far more extravagant spenders than Republicans. At the end of 2008, the debt was about $10 trillion, in itself a national disgrace. Then Mr. Obama took office in January of 2009 and the national debt soared and is now (in 2013) approaching $17 trillion. Among modern presidents, Mr. Obama has been the champion spendthrift, racking up an average deficit of about $1.3 *trillion* per year in office. Figure 9.1 shows the deficit per year in office for President Obama compared to the last three Republican presidents.

During his 2008 campaign, Mr. Obama attacked George W. Bush for the large national debt. Mr. Obama called it unpatriotic and irresponsible. If GW Bush was unpatriotic and irresponsible, how would Mr. Obama characterize his spending excesses?

Figure 9.1 Deficits ($ trillions) per Year in Office
(Comparison of President Obama's deficits to last three Republican Presidents)

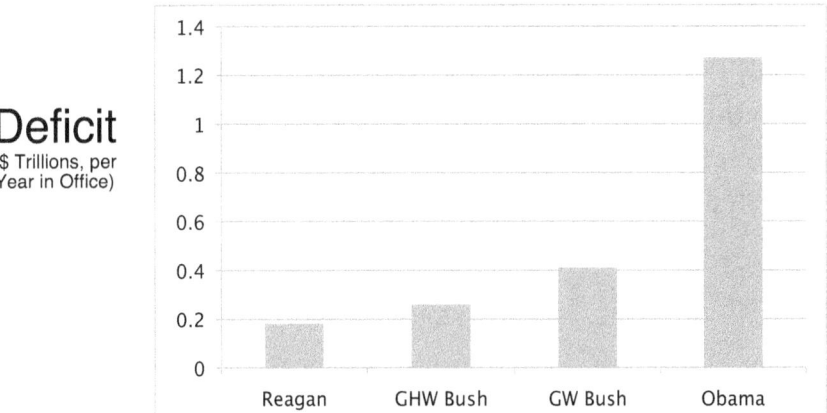

Source: Kimberly Amadeo, http://useconomy.about.com/od/usdebtanddeficit/p/US-Debt-by-President.htm

As noted above, the national debt is now approaching $17 trillion and Congress is considering raising the debt ceiling yet again. The hugeness of that number is difficult to fathom for most Americans and makes eyes glaze over. To put it in perspective, consider this simple exercise: Assume you have $17 trillion and you were to start counting $100 bills at the rate of 1 *per second*. It would require over 5000 *years* to finish, but only if you count 24 hours a day, 365 days per year. Are you up to it?

Let's look at another way to comprehend the enormity of the $17 trillion deficit. First, please consider what a *billion* (10^9) dollars looks like written out: $1,000,000,000. One *trillion* (10^{12}) dollars is $1,000,000,000,000. Even for Washington, that's a lot of money! Imagine for a moment that a *responsible* government has been elected and wants to begin paying off the $17 trillion debt. Assume that this hypothetical administration will squeeze one *billion* dollars *per month* out of the US treasury, rather like you paying your monthly car note. At that rate, America will pay off its debt in the year 3430 AD (or CE if you prefer), or 1417 years from now. How long can such disregard of future generations continue?

In 2012, America paid about $220 billion simply as interest on the debt. That amount of spending ranked fourth in US expenditures, behind only Defense, Medicaid and Medicare. It will probably be much worse in the not-too-distant future because interest rates will inevitably recover from their historic lows. By 2020, the interest on the debt is estimated to run about $1 trillion per year! (2)

Executive Branch

President Obama is suave and projects a very positive public persona. Though he occasionally appears aloof, he is perceived as a good guy, hip, and compassionate. He is articulate and his speeches are usually delivered impeccably. However, as the ancient Greek playwright Sophocles wrote: *It is a terrible thing to speak well and be wrong.*

President Obama prevaricates so smoothly that his audience believes that he must be telling the truth. However, he relies heavily on a teleprompter and has blundered on several occasions without the teleprompter. He is adept at disguising his disdain for the free-market capitalist system and Middle America with soothing words that conceal his contempt. He doesn't simply want to defeat Republicans, he wants to destroy the GOP completely. He can be devious, petty and vindictive, and his demeanor often suggests that he thinks he is above the law. He is narcissistic and prances about, pompously holding his hands just below chest level as he ambles down the steps of Air Force 1. Comedian Dennis Miller described Obama as a "debonair grifter," a near perfect characterization of Mr. Obama (3).

President Obama has by-passed Congress using recess appointments, executive orders (EOs) and regulations issued by his cabinet secretaries, "czars" and agencies. We previously discussed his abuse of power by appointing czars who are not vetted by Congress in Chapter 1. He has seized more power in the executive branch than any president since Franklin Roosevelt.

Recess appointments have historically been used when it is necessary to fill a government position when the Congress is not in session. They have been used by presidents from George Washington to Barack Obama. EOs are also nothing new. All presidents have used them and there is nothing inherently wrong with the practice when used responsibly and judiciously. However, the way Obama has used EOs and recess appointments amounts to legislation by fiat. These practices usurp the role of Congress to provide advice and consent and constitute a breach of the separation of powers. Obama's EOs are reminiscent of imperial decrees or edicts. For example, after he could not get the so-called Dream Act through Congress, President Obama issued an executive order that, in effect, granted amnesty to young illegals brought to the US as children by their parents.

As noted above and briefly discussed in Chapter 1, President Obama has appointed numerous unaccountable czars and has established what can only be called an imperial presidency. And Obama did much of that in his first term when one would think he might have shown restraint considering his intent to run for re-election. Think what he will do now that he no longer needs to be concerned about re-election! In the tradition of Teddy Roosevelt, Woodrow Wilson, and Franklin Roosevelt, Obama will continue to trample the Constitution. He will soon have a leftist-dominated, compliant Supreme Court that will rubber stamp his executive excesses. In 1776, the fledgling USA rejected the excesses of King George III. However, America now has "King Obama."

In his State of the Union address in February of 2013, Obama broadly outlined the investments he planned to make on matters such as green energy. Recall that in Democrat Newspeak, investments mean higher taxes. He also said that "we must do more to combat climate change." Obama arrogantly proclaimed that he would proceed with or without Congress, presumably by using EOs and rules imposed by federal agencies to by-pass Congress. *It's good to be the king* (4).

President Obama's former chief of staff, Rahm Emanuel, made the following comment about government seizing the moment: "You never want a serious crisis to go to waste… it's an opportunity to do things you could not do before" (5). Mr. Obama has used Emanuel's principle. For example, at the very beginning of his presidency in 2009, he signed a huge stimulus program (~$800 billion) intended to alleviate effects of the deep recession. However, a substantial portion of stimulus funds went to wasteful Democrat programs, including subsidies for green energy and electric car companies. It was promised that the stimulus would reduce unemployment. But unemployment remains high, even not counting the thousands of people who have simply given up trying to find a job and are no longer counted as unemployed. Green energy and electric car companies continue to struggle and fail. The economy remains mired in a low growth mode and we'll see, at best, a meager recovery because of the anti-business, anti-fossil fuels policies of President Obama.

EPA and DOJ as Tools of the Executive Branch

Obama's EPA, urged on by environmental activists, has been used to bludgeon businesses with burdensome, costly rules and regulations, particularly the fossil fuel industries. The Heritage Foundation described how the Obama administration has used the EPA and other agencies (6):

> With the help of the Environmental Protection Agency and other departments, this administration has relied on backdoor, behind-the-scenes tactics to impose stringent mandates in order to regulate what it has been unable to legislate. This tactic empowers unelected bureaucrats in Washington to implement rules that have far-reaching, negative impacts on our nation's economy and the way we live our lives.

Department of Justice scandals have occurred such as the *Operation Fast and Furious* fiasco in Mexico and the debacle of the Benghazi cover-up discussed in Chapter 5 which exposed the incompetence of Attorney General Eric Holder. Will the American public ever learn the truth about the four Americans who died in Benghazi?

Local Governments: Big Brother is Alive and Well in NYC and SF

Certain regulations that *impel* citizens to act in a certain way can amount to an infringement on personal liberties. Regrettably, such legislation seems to be on the increase. Some of these laws are in conflict with constitutional rights that *prohibit government* from infringing freedoms of its citizens. This can range from serious matters, such as mandated purchase of health care insurance, to the ridiculous bans of *trans* fat and large soft drinks by Mayor Michael Bloomberg in New

York City. Is it really the role of government to prohibit citizens from imbibing large "sugary" soft drinks?

In Chapter 6, we looked briefly at what happened in San Francisco as a harbinger of what might happen locally because of the global warming boondoggle. In Chapter 8, we opined that political correctness was an underlying reason for the garbage bag ban enacted by the SF city Board of Supervisors. To recap, the Board approved a law in 2007 that bans plastic bags (made from polyethylene) used by grocery stores. (The ban was recently expanded to all retail establishments.) One of the city supervisors complained that discarded plastic bags become eyesores in the community and take up a large amount of space in landfills. As a result, San Franciscans must use reusable cloth bags or pay extra at checkout for "biodegradable" plastic bags, which cost several times that of the plastic bags made from polyethylene. Liberal San Franciscans appear to be pleased with this regulation and apparently embrace it as their civic duty and/or their contribution to saving the environment. However, who is responsible for the trash on the streets of SF? It is the slobs of SF who clutter the environment. If they were more responsible, the "eyesores" of plastic bags would not exist. Moreover, the regulation may not actually solve the problem, since the so-called biodegradable bags will also clutter the roadsides of SF because biodegradation may require months under ambient weather conditions. The remark about lack of landfill space is also bogus (7). While this is admittedly a small matter, it is indicative of what may happen on more consequential issues. It illustrates the trend of Big Brother liberals in government trying to dictate the minutest of citizen behaviors to be more in keeping with leftist worldviews. I fear that the federal government will enact burdensome, costly laws intended to stop global warming.

The Judicial

America's system of jurisprudence has some serious problems. Of course, we humans will never devise a perfect system of justice, but we can do a lot better than what we have now.

The Supreme Court was the last line of defense against the abomination called Obamacare. They failed. After the Court ruled Obamacare to be constitutional, the Congressional Budget Office updated its scoring of the law. The result: Obamacare will cost $1.93 *trillion* over its first decade of existence (2014 to 2023) and leave about 30 million Americans uncovered (8). This is more than twice the original estimate and *is likely to increase even more*. Like many Democrat programs, the essence of Obamacare may be captured in four words: Pay more, get less.

Going back to the late 1970s, liberal presidents have been appointing left-leaning judges to the U.S. judicial system. Indeed, Jimmy Carter appointed a total of 259 federal judges, more in a single term than any other president. Some are still serving (9). A few of these judges have used their powers to legislate from the bench and to reverse the will of the people. Consider, for example, what happened in 1994 in California. Proposition 187 (aka the *Save Our State* petition) was a ballot initiative intended to stop illegal aliens from burdening the state's health care, education system and other social services. The introduction to the proposition stated (10):

> *The People of California find and declare as follows: That they have suffered and are suffering economic hardship caused by the presence of undocumented immigrants in this state. That they have suffered and are suffering personal injury and damage caused by the criminal conduct of undocumented immigrants in this state [and] they have a right to the protection of their government from any person or persons entering this country unlawfully.*

Californians voted overwhelmingly (59% to 41%) in favor of the law. Nevertheless, a federal judge threw out the result, citing that it was unconstitutional and only the federal government could regulate immigration (11). The judge who made the ruling was Mariana Pfaelzer, an appointee of Jimmy Carter.

The ludicrous rulings of the Supreme Court on CO_2 as a pollutant and Obamacare were previously mentioned (Chapters 6 and 3, respectively). The fallout from their ruling on CO_2 has not yet been felt, but it will assuredly cost American businesses dearly. Those added costs will be passed along to the American citizens, in effect a hidden tax. The American consumer will pay more for virtually everything. It will likely begin with increased electricity costs but will cascade into all consumer goods.

The *Roe vs Wade* ruling in 1973 has resulted in the destruction of more than 50 million fetuses, including millions arranged through Planned Parenthood, supported by hundreds of millions of dollars from taxpayers. Were any of those babies destined to become the next Albert Einstein, or a musical genius like Ray Charles, or a brilliant novelist like Michael Crichton? We'll never know. What can be said about a government that refuses to protect its most innocent and vulnerable citizens?

The American civil and criminal justice systems are broken. Frivolous civil lawsuits are clogging the courts. I'm sure most readers recall the famous (or infamous) lawsuit involving hot coffee and McDonald's, described as follows at the website of Legal Zoom (12):

> *In February 1992, Stella Liebeck ordered a cup of coffee to go from McDonalds. Liebeck was sitting in the passenger seat of her nephew's car, which was pulled over so she could add sugar to her coffee. While removing the cup's lid, Liebeck spilled her hot coffee, burning her legs. It was determined that Liebeck suffered third degree burns on over six percent of her body. Originally, Liebeck sought $20,000 in damages. McDonalds refused to settle out of court. However, they should have. Liebeck was ultimately awarded $200,000 in compensatory damages, which was reduced to $160,000 because she was found to be twenty percent at fault. She was also awarded $2.7 million in punitive damages. [emphasis added]*

Though the coffee incident occurred more than 20 years ago, similar awards are still being made. Indeed, awards in the billions have been given in a few cases. I agree fully that people who are harmed because of negligence, malpractice or corporate wrongdoing should receive compensation. However, ludicrous awards such as Ms Liebeck's have been given by juries in an apparent attempt to punish big business. Tort reform is badly needed, but is being vehemently resisted by trial lawyers and leftists.

Judgment by a jury of peers is an antiquated, flawed system. Consider that an obviously guilty O.J. Simpson was acquitted because of jury nullification. The jurors essentially used the verdict as retribution for injustices suffered by African-Americans in the past. Did Nicole Brown Simpson or Ron Goldman receive justice?

Other murderers (*e.g.,* Casey Anthony) have been acquitted by juries that refused to accept the obvious. The left has convinced a sufficient number of Americans that some murderers are not responsible for their actions. It's not their fault. It's because the murderer was abused as a child, or was a victim of spousal battering, or was temporarily insane, or had ADHD or PTSD, etc. Defense lawyers confuse jurors with fanciful explanations that stretch credulity and convince jurors to excuse the inexcusable. It takes only one obstinate juror to hang a jury. Improbable speculations by lawyers are often accepted by jurors to create what they consider to be reasonable doubt. What happened to common sense and personal responsibility?

Juries comprised of people with personal vendettas or people brainwashed by leftist propaganda that excuses any behavior will continue to render unjust verdicts. Something should be done to minimize miscarriages of justice in the US civil and criminal justice systems. But what? Regardless of reforms enacted, errors will still occur. I realize that no system devised by humankind will ever be perfect. Nevertheless, regarding the present system as sacrosanct seems to me an admission that occasional unjust verdicts are acceptable.

Congress

The careless attitude of Democrats toward money and budgets is evident in their neglect of the constitutional requirement that the Senate present a budget before February each year. As I write this in early 2013, the Democrat-controlled Senate has not passed a budget since April of 2009. Ignoring the budget process is an example of Democrats' disregard of a Constitutional requirement. Much of the blame can be laid at the feet of current Senate Majority Leader Harry Reid (D-NV). Reid's lack of leadership has relegated the country to budget by continuing resolutions and appropriation bills for several years. When Obama proposed a budget early in 2012, it was defeated in the senate 99-0 and 414-0 in the House of Representatives (13). Not a single Democrat in either house would vote for Obama's budget!

Twice during 2012, polls showed disapproval of Congress by the American public reached an all-time low of 10% (14). The American public is well aware of the incompetence that is all too common in Congress.

Sheila Jackson-Lee (D-TX) has been elected and re-elected to the US House of Representatives for 9 terms. Though Democrats have many less than illustrious members of Congress, Ms Jackson-Lee is in a class by herself. She is among the most inept and uninformed members of Congress, even worse than present and former Congressional Democrats Nancy Pelosi (D-CA), Alan Grayson (D-FL), Cynthia McKinney (D-GA), Jim McDermott (D-WA), Anthony Weiner (D-NY) and Maxine Waters (D-CA). While touring the Jet Propulsion Lab in California, Representative Jackson-Lee asked whether the American flag planted by Neil Armstrong was still visible on the surface of Mars (15). Representative Jackson-Lee also suggested that it was discriminatory that names assigned to Tropical Storms and Hurricanes did not include African-American names. Bernie Goldberg facetiously suggested that affirmative action be applied to naming storms and names such as Keisha, Jamal, DeShawn or LaToya should be used (16).

After the Boston Marathon bombing in April of 2013, Ms Jackson-Lee suggested that it was, in part, because of budget cuts caused by the sequester (except she pronounced it "sekester.") Do you feel more comfortable knowing that people like Jackson-Lee, Weiner, McDermott, Grayson and Waters are determining the direction of America? Are you ready to reconsider the question raised in Chapter 7 about whether the ignorant should be allowed to vote? How can America do anything but decay when people like these are casting votes in Congress?

Chapter 10

WHERE DO WE GO FROM HERE?

There is no cure for birth and death save to enjoy the interval.

George Santayana

Life Goes On

L IKE MANY CONSERVATIVE AMERICANS, I was bitterly disappointed and discouraged by the re-election of extreme leftist Barack Obama. Indeed, this book is a direct consequence of trying to understand how Mr. Obama could have been re-elected. Results of my analysis suggest that, unless voting patterns change, conservatism and the Republican Party are headed toward irrelevance, especially after the midpoint of the 21st century. I believe Obama's re-election was symptomatic of the ongoing decline of America. However, as the Beatles told us in the late 1960s, life goes on. The sun will rise tomorrow and we will still have to get up, go to work and pay our bills. Though the country will be diminished, we'll get past it. The country survived leftists Woodrow Wilson, Lyndon Johnson and Jimmy Carter and it will survive Barack Obama, at least for the medium-term. Unfortunately, America will continue its slide toward becoming a centrally controlled European-style Nanny State.

In the interim, conservatives who oppose socialism will have to pick themselves up, dust themselves off and resume the fight. We can't give up or the decay will proceed even faster. The economy will eventually recover in spite (not because) of President Obama. It will probably be a pathetically weak recovery, but a recovery nonetheless. It will occur for the most part owing to the cyclical nature of business and the resilience of the American people. However, the lapdog mainstream media will credit Mr. Obama with the inevitable resurgence of the economy. Important elements of their cover for Obama will be to convince Americans that a weak economy and 7-8% unemployment are the "new normal." Obama's misguided policies on energy will make everything cost more, far above the normal rate of inflation. It will eventually force Americans to make difficult life-style choices (if, indeed, choices are still allowed) on what they can afford (electric or

ICE car? Window fans or air-conditioning? Fluorescent light bulbs or candles? …and so on, *ad nauseam*.)

The decline will not be precipitous and the US should be able to adapt to its diminished influence. Observe what happened to the British Empire. Though I am an unabashed Anglophile, it must be acknowledged that Great Britain is not the dominating global force it once was; it has receded from a position of supremacy in the 18th and 19th centuries. Nevertheless, it remains respected and highly influential in world events. Their language has become the dominant language of the world, much to the chagrin of the French. English citizens rightly take great pride in its magnificent history. The indomitable British people will forever have a claim to the moral high ground for their valiant resistance in 1940-41, when they stood alone against Hitler's tyranny.

I recently had occasion to spend a few days in India. If there's anything that will make you realize how fortunate we are to live in America, it's observing the grinding poverty of the long-suffering people of India. It renewed my appreciation of the wonders that free market capitalism, individual liberties and the entrepreneurial spirit of the American people have wrought in the US. Unfortunately, too many Americans take our marvelous free-market capitalist system for granted. Some from the left are even trying to destroy it.

Again risking being accused of jingoism, I think America is the greatest country in the history of humankind and, until recently, I believed that it would continue indefinitely. But, as posited in this book, I fear that America is well on its way to becoming a centrally controlled Orwellian socialist state. That will destroy American exceptionalism. I do not believe that America's demise will occur because of violent revolution, but rather from incremental decay owing to liberal policies and citizen apathy. Too many Americans are simply not paying attention. Many citizens remain oblivious, but they continue to cast ignorant votes, thereby allowing forces from the left "to fundamentally transform" America.

I am not suggesting a vast left-wing conspiracy, to paraphrase Hillary Clinton. However, certain policies and agencies established by Teddy Roosevelt and Woodrow Wilson and propagated by subsequent liberal presidents are slowly eating away the very foundations of traditional American self-sufficiency and system of governance. For example, Lyndon Johnson's *War on Poverty* and his socialistic *Great Society Program* were miserable failures. Obamacare, as presently structured, will also be a costly failure.

Some are calling for a major revamping of the Republican Party. They apparently want the GOP to soften conservative positions to accommodate the changing demographics of the country. For example, some suggest trying to capture more of the Hispanic vote by adopting more lenient stances on illegal immigration. This may require the Republican Party to move closer to the liberal positions of the Democrat Party. That is, the GOP may become the "Democrat-lite" Party. America doesn't need another Democrat Party!

Unless some of the less ideological in the Democrat coalition discussed in Chapter 3 wise up, Republicans will find it increasingly difficult to be elected. Several factions in the Democrat coalition are intransigent and will forsake their liberal principles only after hell freezes over. However, it may be possible to persuade the more rational Democrat factions to vote for conservatism. Unfortunately, practicality, individual responsibility and fiscal sanity are much harder to sell than the utopia and freebies promised in the fantasy world of Democrats. For too many Americans today, instant gratification trumps discipline and fiscal responsibility and to hell with the consequences.

Nevertheless, Republican presidents will still occasionally be elected, at least up to the mid-point of the 21st century, because even an uninformed electorate will tire of leftist excesses. Perhaps a rising young Republican might be elected in 2016. The Republican Party has several young candidates who might save the country from the catastrophe of a Hillary Clinton or Joe Biden presidency, including Rand Paul, Marco Rubio, Alan West, Susana Martinez, Paul Ryan, Ted Cruz and Bobby Jindal. Indeed, it may be someone else who will burst on the scene as Obama did in 2008. Almost any conservative would be a better President than Hillary Clinton. However, as we shall see in the next section, Republicans will find it nearly impossible to be elected in the latter half of the 21st century, unless there are substantial shifts in how blocs of Americans vote.

Elections in 2052 and Beyond

The USA Today reported the following shortly after the November 6, 2012 election (1):

> Barack Obama won just over 50% of the popular vote last week, but he earned 80% of non-white votes and about 39% of white votes. According to USA Today exit poll data, he secured 93% of the Black vote, 73% of the Asian vote, 71% of the Hispanic vote, and 58% of the non-white [o]ther vote.

In 2050, when my grandchildren have become middle-aged (and, as my "grandies" callously remind me, I will be dead), the demographic mix in the US is projected to be (2):

47% White
29% Hispanic
13% African-American
9% Asian

Let's look at possible implications of these demographic projections for the 2052 election of President. For purposes of calculation, let's assume that the 2% balance is "other non-white" and that Americans vote in proportions comparable to their demographic percentages. Using the demographic projections from above and voting patterns from the 2012 election, we can calculate the anticipated vote for the Democrat candidate in 2052 as follows:

$$47(0.39) + 29(0.73) + 13(0.93) + 9(0.73) + 2(0.58) = 59.3$$

In other words, assuming that the demographic groups identified above vote as they did in 2012, the Democrat candidate will capture just over **59%** of the vote! (I also calculated the expected vote for the Democrat adjusting for turnout of each demographic group using data from the 2012 election. The result was that the Democrat received about 58%, only slightly less than above.) Clearly, *unless voting patterns change*, a Republican candidate is very unlikely to be elected in 2052 and beyond.

Let's look at another scenario. If one assumes that 50.1% of the vote is sufficient to elect a candidate as we saw in Chapter 3, using the percentages above and the projected demographic mix for 2050, the Democrat need only receive 33.4%, or one in three, white votes to be elected.

Let's examine one last scenario for the 2052 presidential election. For this example, except for the so-called "white vote," we'll again assume that demographic groups vote as they did in 2012. To defeat the Democrat candidate, the Republican would have to receive *at least* 87% of the white vote, a remote possibility.

Demographic trends in America suggest that conservatives will constitute a smaller and smaller segment of the populace. What is to become of conservatives who don't wish to abandon their principles? It is my belief that forming a third party is not the answer, at least not in the near term. How many Libertarians have been elected to national office? In the 2012 presidential election the Libertarian candidate received only about 1% of the popular vote.

It is my opinion that the best course for conservatives is to remain in the Republican Party. However, it will be imperative that the GOP capture a larger share of the so-called independent vote. Also, portions of the Democrat factions that are less dogmatically bound to liberal ideology will need to be convinced to vote for conservatives. Perhaps some of the moron vote can be educated to the point where they understand that it is not in the best interests of themselves or America to continue electing leftists. Other possible targets are the oblivious white vote and the youth vote. It is even possible that more African-Americans might be convinced to repudiate the empty promises of the left. (After all, they need only observe the pathetic condition of the cities of Washington D.C. and Detroit after 50+ years of uninterrupted governance by liberal Democrats.) Perhaps a larger percentage of Hispanics can also be convinced to vote for conservatives. Stereotypes of Republicans as uncaring, mean, bigoted, rich people have to be corrected. Without such changes, the Republican Party will become irrelevant in national elections in the latter half of the 21st century.

How can these potential voters be turned to the GOP? Though it will not be easy, it is not impossible. It will require educating these voters. It will require conveying the conservative message in a *positive* way, all the while fighting the vitriol, distortions and misinformation spread by the mainstream media, academia, Hollywood elitists and clueless entertainers and celebrities.

We who believe in limited government, free market capitalism, individual liberties, strong defense and low taxes will prevail in some future elections, at least up until the middle of the 21st century. Americans will reject government dictating every aspect of their lives, perhaps as soon as 2016. However, I doubt that the damages inflicted by liberals over the past century can be reversed anytime soon. For example, Obamacare is probably here to stay.

History teaches us that empires come and go, though it may have seemed that they would last forever during their heyday. Long ago, the Mongolian Empire of Genghis Khan, the Persian Empire, and the Roman Empire ran their courses, but eventually declined. In more recent times, the Ottoman Empire ended early in the 20th century, Hitler's Third Reich was comprehensively destroyed in World War II and communist USSR collapsed from within in 1991. Empires dominate the world for awhile, then fade into mediocrity or even completely disappear. Just as there are cycles in life, sports and weather, there are cycles in countries that dominate the world. America is dying and the best we can hope for in the near-to-medium term is that thinking citizens will realize the damage being done by liberals and reject leftism. Longer term (after the mid-point of the 21st century), America will be saved from perpetual leftist governments only if substantial changes in voting patterns occur.

As suggested above, Democrats will probably dominate national politics in the latter half of the 21st century. What will happen when leftists have everything their way? Big Brother and the Thought Police will be in charge. Personal liberties will be greatly curtailed and certain freedoms will have gone the way of the dinosaur. You may be required to buy an electric car or perhaps a hybrid in the effort to save the world from "global warming." You may be paying $6/gal or more for gasoline much sooner than normal inflation would dictate. Lawn mowers will have to be electric. Utility companies will be so thoroughly regulated and taxed that your electricity bills will be enormous. Many will not be able to afford air-conditioning for their homes. Bicycles and scooters may become primary means of transport. The government will select your doctor and, when you become elderly, a bureaucratic government panel may decide that you're too old for a life-saving operation. (As Mr. Obama famously suggested, the elderly may be told to take a pill.) You will be prohibited from consuming *trans* fat and large sugary soft drinks, if leftist politicians like New York Mayor Bloomberg are able to pronounce what is acceptable.

How can the decline be stopped? I don't think it can. However, that doesn't mean that the country will cease to exist anytime soon. The US will not disintegrate overnight. After all, it took over a century of misguided leftist policies to bring us to this point. Though liberals will continue to chip away at American exceptionalism, they will do it bit-by-bit, as they have since the days of Woodrow Wilson. The incremental slippage of America to a second rate power may barely be noticed. But America will become less and less relevant in world events. One day, citizens will look up and realize that China has replaced America as the world's foremost superpower. I earnestly hope that day is far in the future.

What can be done to improve the situation and postpone the inevitable? Several things come immediately to mind:

➤ The US economy is on life support and must be resuscitated. The sad state of the economy was caused by years of wrongheaded policies and purposeful damage inflicted by Mr. Obama and other leftists. We cannot continue with growth rates of ~2% as we had in 2011 and 2012. As mentioned earlier, the economy will improve in spite of Mr. Obama, but it will be a meager recovery. A great place to jump start the economy is in the fossil fuels industries. America should develop domestic oil, natural gas and coal, including on federal lands such as ANWR. Open offshore fields to oil and natural gas development. These measures will not only benefit the country economically by creating thousands of jobs, but will also improve national security.

➤ Fracking to obtain natural gas and oil should proceed without government interference. Fossil fuels will continue to be vital to America well into the 21st century, even if viable alternatives are discovered. Misinformation spread by antihumanists and Hollywood elitists should not be allowed to prevent fracking.

➤ Do something about the national debt! As I write this, America's debt is climbing toward $17 trillion and it is projected to be around $20 trillion by the time Mr. Obama leaves office! As a beginning, the US government must stop overspending. In 2012, $220 billion went just to pay the interest on the debt; in 2020, it is expected to be $1 trillion! (3). That is a shameful legacy to leave our grandchildren and great grandchildren.

➤ Require all voters to produce a photo ID. This should reduce voter fraud and improve the integrity of the electoral process. Further, other than those in poverty, only income tax-paying citizens of the US should be allowed to vote. Additionally, voter rolls should be periodically purged of people who have moved out of the area or passed away. (I know it's already something that supposed to happen, but it's not being done. Otherwise, dead people would not be voting!)

➤ At the risk of being called a snob, I agree with the liberal LZ Granderson (4). He and I believe that the ignorant should not be allowed to vote, until they are able to demonstrate a minimal understanding of American civics and US history. People have to pass a driving test before being granted a driver's license. Just as ignorant, unlicensed drivers might injure other motorists, ignorant voters can inflict harm on their fellow citizens.

➤ Completely overhaul the tax code. There is no way that nearly half of US wage-earners should pay zero income tax! Is it fair that 100% of income taxes are paid by 52% of wage-earners? I don't think so. Though I have no issue with the progressive tax tables, the tables need complete restructuring. Spreading the burden of taxes across a broader spectrum of the populace may impel voters to pay more attention as to how the government is spending their money. Increasing the number of voters having "skin in the game" can only help conservatives.

➤ Stop wasting billions trying to prevent global warming, which is going to happen, whether or not government imposes carbon taxes or other punitive measures. Some of those billions saved should be used to reduce the national debt or for research to solve truly meaningful problems, like developing improved antibiotics.

➤ Support R&D to develop alternatives to fossil fuels, but stop subsidies to suspect green energy companies. The Solyndra episode must not be repeated. Also, government should not mandate that citizens purchase all or part of their electricity produced by wind or solar. Rather, those technologies should become more cost-effective and succeed in the marketplace on their own merits.

> Stop the "ethanol as fuel" boondoggle. It's a waste of money rooted in the drive to become independent of Middle Eastern Oil and the myth of *man-caused* global warming. Not only is it of dubious value, it distorts markets for farm products and *is harmful to the poor when food crops are diverted to uses other than feeding the masses.*

> Though development of alternative fuels for internal combustion engines is a thorny issue, it can be solved. As noted above, ethanol is not the answer. On the other hand, methanol is a promising, practical alternative and deserves serious consideration (5).

> Stop subsidizing companies manufacturing the *total* electric cars, which today are impractical and overly expensive. Though support for research should continue, subsidies for manufacturers are a waste of taxpayer money and will continue to be so, until deficiencies mentioned in Chapter 4 are overcome.

> Social Security and Medicare programs must be reformed. For example, it is perfectly reasonable, in view of today's longer life expectancies, to increase the age for eligibility for social security *gradually* up to 70. Further, the proposal to allow social security participants to manage at least a portion of their money in self-directed investments should become law. It is irrational for Democrats to oppose such common sense measures.

I recognize that most of these suggestions will be given short shrift by leftists. That is unfortunate, because these measures would buy more time for America.

I suggested in Chapter 1 that America is on a path to becoming a second rate Nanny-state, like France and other European countries.

Becoming more French-like will not be viewed favorably by many Americans. In recent times, large numbers of American and French citizens have expressed an intense mutual dislike. Many Americans consider the French to be snooty, ethnocentric, pusillanimous elitists. The French generally regard America as a cultural wasteland and the American people as boorish, ill-mannered cretins. While France and America are nominally allies, the contempt, scorn and animus between their citizens are palpable. It hasn't always been that way. Early Americans were thankful for the contributions of Frenchman Lafayette during the Revolutionary War. The magnificent Statue of Liberty, a gift from the people of France to commemorate the US centennial, has become an iconic symbol of American freedom.

Looking on the bright side, America becoming like France has some positives. The French are a proud people who truly know how to enjoy life. The French have the best cuisine in the world. Some of the world's most brilliant scientists have been French (Pasteur, Descartes, Barbier, Grignard and Curie). Unlike Americans, the French have made the highly intelligent and practical choice to embrace nuclear energy. Becoming more like France would mean that America would no longer have to be the world's policeman. Even Democrats might lower taxes, since America will no longer have to maintain the world's most formidable armed forces. America may never again have to suffer Pyrrhic victories in war, as it did during my father's generation on Iwo Jima, Okinawa and Omaha Beach. America has always been a compassionate, generous country and we will never abandon our role in relieving misery in the world. We can *help* the English, French, Dutch and Germans stop atrocities committed by African warlords and to feed the starving in Somalia, Sudan or Ethiopia. However, like the Euro states, we can otherwise withdraw behind our borders and concentrate on making excellent cheeses and whines to rival the French.

Why, you ask, don't leftists simply move to a country that is already closer to socialist paradise? It's too late for them to move to the USSR, but there's still North Korea and Cuba. China and Vietnam don't count because they allow too much capitalism for most social-ists. (And yes, I know the answer to the question above: Leftists want to remain here to change America into their vision of utopia, whether the rest of us want socialism or not.)

Secession?

Over the years, there have been numerous proposals _within_ states for secession to form a 51st state (6). For example, as recently as 2008, a proposal was made for Long Island to secede from the state of New York. Over its history, California has considered a variety of seces-sion plans to divide into separate states (_e.g._, the state of "Southern California" [7]).

More recently, officials from eight counties in northern Colorado have discussed the possibility of secession (8).

Another alternative is for leftists in hopelessly blue states to secede from the USA altogether and form their own countries. For example, the like-minded states of Washington and Oregon could consolidate and form the _United States of the Pacific_. Other names might better capture their political leanings:

> _The Union of Socialist Republics of the Pacific_
> _The Peoples Republic of Pacific States_

A country called _Cascadia_ has already been proposed, which would include Washington and Oregon, but also included part of British Columbia (7). I suspect Canada might not support the forma-tion of _Cascadia_.

According to a book by the late Thomas Naylor, secession is not prohibited by the US Constitution (9). Naylor's book, published in 2008, is entitled _Secession_ with the subtitle: _How Vermont and All the Other States Can Save Themselves from the Empire_ .The Manifesto from his book began:

Thoughtful Vermonters opposed to the tyranny of the United States government, Corporate America, and globalization, believe that Vermont should once again become an independent republic... and that the United States should begin to peacefully dissolve [sic].

Naylor's book is vociferously leftist (what else would you expect from Vermont?). He was an intolerant anti-American, anti-big business, anti-Israel liberal. He was a great admirer of socialist countries such as Switzerland and Sweden. He was a firm believer in the anthropogenic global warming myth and harbored an intense hatred for George W. Bush and America. He probably voted numerous times for the socialist Bernie Sanders. You might suspect that he would be a devout Democrat, but he was very negative on the Democrat Party. In fact, he claimed that there is little difference between the Democrat and Republican parties and that, effectively, America has only one party (The Republican Party). Perhaps you might be surprised that I share a few opinions with the late Mr. Naylor about the Democrat Party and what he called the American Empire. Consider these passages from his Manifesto:

...The comatose Democratic Party is effectively brain dead, having had no new ideas since the 1960s...

...in addition to being too big, our [American] government is too centralized, too powerful, too intrusive, too materialistic and too unresponsive to the needs of individual citizens and small communities...

However, I strongly disagree with almost all of the other positions of Mr. Naylor. While I mourn the decline of America, the late Mr. Naylor would probably have rejoiced.

Naylor believed that Vermont's citizens are superior to people from other states. Naylor had an especially condescending opinion of

Southerners, as is evident from his bigoted statement related to the secession of Vermont:

> *Secession is a very tough sell, particularly in New England, where everyone knows that only redneck racists from the South believe in secession.*

Mr. Naylor clearly believed in secession. Should we then conclude that the late Mr. Naylor was a "redneck racist"?

From a personal standpoint, I sincerely hope that Vermont is able to depart the Union. The Second Vermont Republic will be a true socialist paradise. The SVR deserves to have Howard Dean as president. I wish them luck with their electric cars, wind turbines and solar cells. Also, I wish Vermonters good luck building a global economy based on ski resorts, organic vegetables and Ben & Jerry's ice cream.

It is obvious that different parts of the country have irreconcilable differences. The chasm between left and right (or red and blue states) is becoming vast and the country may be unable to bridge it. Perhaps the time *has* come to consider an amicable parting of ways.

Conclusion

As I approach the end of this book, I think about my grandchildren and great grandchildren yet to be born. I fear that recent generations (including my own) have made voting decisions about American government that are leaving our progeny a shameful legacy. On behalf of my contemporaries, I apologize to our descendants for the sorry state of the country that we bequeath to them.

As noted earlier, nearly half of the wage-earners in America today don't pay any income tax. When you rob Peter to pay Paul, Paul rarely complains. America simply has too many Pauls. When you have more takers than contributors, the system will ultimately collapse. That is the inevitable downfall of democracy. Lord Thomas B. Macaulay expressed a similar idea more than 250 years ago and it is fitting to consider his thought as we near the conclusion of this book (10):

> *A democracy cannot survive as a permanent form of government. It can last only until its citizens discover that they can vote themselves largesse from the public treasury. From that moment on, the majority will vote for the candidates promising the greatest benefits from the public purse, with the result that a democracy will always collapse from loose fiscal policies...*

Unfortunately, America has chosen the path of "loose fiscal policies" by electing leftists like Wilson, FDR, LBJ and Obama over the past century. President Obama's spending has increased the national debt to nearly $17 *trillion* and Obamacare implementation will cost trillions more.

I have entered the winter of my life and will be little affected personally by the further decline of America. However, I regret that my descendants will have to suffer the consequences. Nevertheless, it's been cathartic for me to write this tome. I considered it a chance to speak from beyond to my progeny about the greatness of this country in days of yore. It provided an opportunity for me to explain my view of what went wrong and how the inevitable may be postponed. Notwithstanding the bleak outlook for America, I conclude this book by echoing the sentiment expressed by Abraham Lincoln as he closed his unforgettable Gettysburg Address: ...*that government of the people, by the people, for the people, shall not perish from the earth.* I take my leave with this poignant statement; it captures my most earnest hope for America.

EPILOGUE

As this book was being completed in May of 2013, the Obama administration was wracked by a series of scandals having to do with the Benghazi attacks, IRS targeting of conservative organizations and Department of Justice malfeasance against journalists, including possible abrogation of the First Amendment right to a free press. Embattled Attorney General Eric Holder appears to have been involved in the DOJ scandal to an as-yet undetermined extent. Holder is further believed to have perjured himself before Congress and calls for his resignation are increasing. Will the mainstream media, at long last, try to uncover answers? At this point, most of the media are either downplaying or avoiding coverage of these stories altogether. Will they give the Obama administration another pass? Unless the mainstream media succeeds in burying these stories, they will remain in the news for weeks, or even months, after this book is published.

I considered revising segments of the book having to do with corruption and incompetence in the Obama administration, especially in Chapters 5 and 9. However, I decided against an extensive rewrite, because I didn't want the extra work and recent revelations have not materially changed essential points about the Obama administration. After reviewing what was written about Benghazi in Chapter 5, for example, I concluded that little needed to be revised. At this point, questions raised in Chapter 5 remained unanswered. What is new is the testimony given by "whistleblowers" who recently came forward and were questioned about the September 11, 2012 terrorist attack in Benghazi. They disclosed information about the attacks that raised serious concerns about the veracity of the Obama administration.

There have also been developments are in the energy arena. After more than 3 years of obstruction and delays, rumors indicate that President Obama may finally approve the Keystone XL Pipeline mentioned in Chapter 4. A final decision is to be announced later in 2013. However, at the same time, Mr. Obama's Department of Interior is imposing many new regulations and rules on the fracking industry. (Obama giveth and he taketh away.)

The quandary in which America finds itself today is exacerbated by the issue of illegal immigrants (or undocumented workers, if you prefer the PC term). However, this topic is not even broached in the body of this book. Illegal immigration is an issue that is firmly rooted in the left-right dichotomy and for which easy solutions do not exist. In general, leftists appear to support policies tantamount to open borders and general amnesty for illegal immigrants. (Not surprising, since most illegals are Hispanic and Democrats typically receive >70% of the Hispanic vote.) The right is concerned that such policies will undermine America and will be a danger to the sovereignty of the country, not to mention the burden that millions of illegal immigrants will impose upon on America. Another concern is that porous borders may allow terrorists (Islamic or otherwise) to enter the country undetected.

I do not presume to have a solution to the illegal immigration/amnesty conundrum. However, I do have a few annoyances about illegal immigration that I'd like to mention. Immigration and Customs Enforcement (ICE) personnel are trying valiantly to hold the line against illegal immigration along our southern border. However, Washington regards border security to be solely a federal responsibility and refuses to seek local or state assistance. (It's almost as if the federal government doesn't truly want to stop illegal immigration.) A good first step to improve border security would be to insure that federal, state and local personnel work together. Another priority should be to build more effective barriers to make it much more difficult to cross the border illegally. This could be achieved with higher fences, more extensive use of electronic surveillance, drones, helicopters, infrared cameras, etc. It seems fundamental that if you stop most of the illegal crossings, you have prevented the problem from becoming even larger. With the border secure, you can turn your attention to the 11+ million illegal immigrants already here.

Another peeve is this: The illegal immigrant appears to have little fear of being apprehended, because the consequences are so lenient. For example, let's assume that ICE has apprehended Señor Juan Valdez, the erstwhile coffee farmer from Columbia, trying to enter the country illegally. As I understand the process now, since Señor Valdez is not a terrorist, he would typically have to pay a small fine and then be deported, a mere slap on the wrist. However, Señor Valdez may return and try again to sneak across the border. If captured once more, he is again fined but, though he could receive a lengthy prison term, in most cases, after a short stay in jail, he is simply deported again. This appears to be a never-ending game of "hide-and-seek." With the easy availability of computer records and modern DNA technology, it should be quite easy to detect repeat offenders. It's now the 21st century! Why don't repeat offenders suffer more substantial consequences? Perhaps first-time offenders could be held in detention centers, but repeat offenders could receive automatic jail time, with incarceration time increasing with each apprehension. I realize that life in an American jail might be cushy for someone from south of the border. Nevertheless, the offender is incarcerated and is unable to cross the border again until his jail time is served. If more effective barriers are put in place, as suggested above, there will be fewer illegal crossings (SECURE THE BORDER FIRST!). Fewer crossings will result in fewer illegal immigrants being apprehended. The liberal complaint about overcrowded jails should become moot, since effective barriers will dramatically reduce the number of illegals apprehended and incarcerated. The left will still register their usual objections (racism, inhumane treatment, lack of medical care, etc.), but they should be fewer.

An additional complaint about immigration has to do with Section 1 of the 14th Amendment which states that children born in the US automatically become citizens. The 14th Amendment was adopted in 1868 and had more to do with reversing the Supreme Court's decision on the Dred Scott law of 1866 (1). The 14th Amendment has been interpreted to mean that children become US citizens, even if their parents are in the country illegally. This policy constitutes another magnet for illegal immigrants. Though it is an outdated, harebrained law, chances of repeal are slim to none, and slim just left town. Not a single European country has a law like it (2). Also, Australia and New Zealand both recently repealed similar laws. Section 1 of the 14th Amendment should be repealed or at least revised, such that only children of *legal* immigrants automatically become US citizens. Since repeal will occur a few days after hell freezes over, resolution of the illegal immigration problem will have to be done using the aforementioned measures: better border security and more severe punishments for violators.

Another topic that I should mention has to do with the ongoing decline of Europe. That subject was only peripheral to the principal points of this book. Nevertheless, I alluded several times to the socialistic Nanny States that have become prevalent in Europe. Mark Steyn's book *America Alone* contains excellent discussions about what has happened in Europe. Steyn opines that Europe is dying, but he contends that America isn't (3). Of course, I disagree, and have suggested in this book that America is also dying because of leftist influences on government over the past century. Steyn touches on Muslim assimilation, birth rates and demography and the consequences for Europe, which are going to be dire. Steyn's brilliant, witty writing is wonderfully entertaining, but has a very serious underlying message: America may be the last bastion of western civilization.

A basic tenet of this book is that America's ongoing drift to the left is destroying the country, though incurable leftists will probably welcome America's conversion into a socialist state. From the recent scandals in the Obama administration to the ridiculous antics of the global warming loons, current events are replete with examples of liberal insanity and incompetence. Just watch the local news and an unbiased version of the national news and you'll see ample evidence of America in decline.

CHAPTER NOTES

Chapter 1 Change, Liberals and the Mainstream Media

1. After the lighting went out at the Super Dome in New Orleans during the 2013 Super Bowl, FEMA issued the following statement (see post at *palookavillepost.com* › *City Hall* › *US Politics*:

   President George Bush's failure to lift a finger to help the impoverished people of New Orleans before, during and after Hurricane Katrina is the root cause of the power outage at yesterday's Super Bowl extravaganza. Corrosion in a nearby transformer caused a breaker switch to open, shutting off power to much of the stadium.

2. S. D. Alinsky, *Rules for Radicals*, Vintage Books (Division of Random House), **1971**.

3. A. Napolitano, *Theodore and Woodrow*, Thomas Nelson Inc., **2012**.

4. "American exceptionalism" is an oft-used term but is widely misunderstood. The term is not intended to suggest that Americans are superior to people from other countries. President Obama's concept of the term became evident when he said "I believe in American exceptionalism, just as I suspect that the Brits believe in British exceptionalism and the Greeks believe in Greek exceptionalism." Every country can't be exceptional. Does Obama think that Turkmenistanis believe in "Turkmenistani exceptionalism"?

Perhaps, but have the Turkmenistanis put a man on the moon? Did they invent the light bulb, the Internet or computers? Can they build aircraft like the Boeing 787 Dreamliner? "American exceptionalism" is a result of the American system of government and individual freedoms that, as this book contends, have been under assault by leftists for more than a century. From the Wikipedia article: "...America's exceptionalism stems from its emergence from a revolution... to become independent and developing a uniquely American ideology, based on liberty, egalitarianism, individualism, populism and laissez-faire." Because of leftist policies that infringe on the free enterprise system and individual liberties, "American exceptionalism" is becoming a thing of the past. As some leftists hope, Americans may indeed become more like the Turkmenistanis. "Chinese exceptionalism" or "Japanese exceptionalism" may replace American exceptionalism.

5. It is perfectly reasonable to ask why dissatisfied leftists don't simply move to countries that fulfill their concept of societal perfection. Of course, most would answer that they want to transform America into Utopia. Unfortunately, they are destroying America. They are making conservative Americans want to move to another country that is less hampered by the plague of leftism. How about Australia? How about the Czech Republic, whose late president Vaclav Havel was one of few European high officials who recognized the anthropogenic global warming boondoggle and the blatant politicization of the IPCC? (See Chapter 6.)

6. Taken from a speech (on April 3, 2009) by President Obama in Strasbourg, France as posted by Robert Farley at FactCheck.org on August 31, 2012:

"I know that there have been honest disagreements over policy, but we also know that there's something more that has crept into our relationship. In America, there's a failure to appreciate Europe's leading role in the world.

Instead of celebrating your dynamic union and seeking to partner with you to meet common challenges, there have been times where America has shown arrogance and been dismissive, even derisive."

7. A. Napolitano, *Theodore and Woodrow*, Thomas Nelson Inc., 82, **2012**.

8. Obama appointed 38 people to positions that are intended to focus on various aspects of governance in his first term, more than any other president. Often, they are called "czars," but the Obama administration assigned titles they apparently believed to be more appropriate. Czars deal with administration policies related to matters such as green energy, drugs, ethics, cyber security, compensation, climate change, Asian carp, domestic violence, war, urban affairs, economic, etc. en.wikipedia.org/wiki/List_of_U.S._executive_branch_czars.

9. George Zimmerman, a volunteer community-watch participant in Florida, was arrested for the murder of Trayvon Martin. His audiotape call to 911 was edited by NBC in a selective way that made it appear that Zimmerman was racist. In fact, he was simply replying to a question from the 9-1-1 operator. See, for example, www.npr.org/blogs/thetwo-way/2012/04/11/150449405/zimmerman-arrested-on-murder-charge-in-martin-case. Several NBC employees (including a producer) were fired over the incident. In December, 2012, Zimmerman filed suit against NBC.

10. B. Goldberg, *Bias*, Regnery Publishing, Inc., **2002**.

11. B. Goldberg, *Arrogance*, Warner Books, Inc., **2003**.

12. A. Coulter, *Slander*, Three Rivers Press, **2002**.

13. A. Coulter, *Treason*, Three Rivers Press, **2003.**

14. A. Coulter, *Guilty*, Crown Publishing, **2008**.

15. B. Goldberg, *100 People Who Are Screwing Up America (and Al Franken is #37)*, HarperCollins Publishers, **2005.**

16. Harris, Sheldon H., *Factories of Death, Japanese Biological Warfare and the American Cover-up*, Routledge, **2002**; see

also Williams, Peter, and Wallace, David, *Unit 731:Japan's Secret Biological Warfare in World War II,* Free Press, **1989**. These books are among several about horrific human experimentation, including vivisection, used by the Japanese on prisoners (mostly Chinese, but including a few American POWs) in the Ping Fan prison near Harbin, Manchuria during the 1930s and 1940s.

Chapter 2 Progressivism and Neocommunism

1. This phrase is derived from an observation about socialism attributed to the late Margaret Thatcher, "The Iron Lady" and Prime Minister of the United Kingdom from 1979 to 1990. Though slightly different wording has been reported, the following captures the sentiment of what Ms Thatcher said: "Socialism works great until you run out of other peoples' money."

2. The Venona project was the classified name for an American cryptologic code breaking program from the 1940s. The deciphered messages were declassified in 1995. They show unequivocally that hundreds of communists in the US were indeed delivering secrets to the USSR, including Julius Rosenberg and several high-placed US government officials.

3. D. Sirota post from March 25, 2010; truthdig.com/.../the_difference_between_liberalism_and_**progressivism** _20100325/; see also *The Progressive Review, http://prorev.com/proglib.htm*

4. Will, George, *Washington Post,* December 19, 2010.

5. *en.wikipedia.org/wiki/Nancy_Jacobson*

6. Franken, Al, *Rush Limbaugh is a Big Fat Idiot,* Dell Publishing, **1996.**

7. Bryce, Robert, *Gusher of Lies,* PublicAffairs, **2008**; Bryce, Robert, *Power Hungry,* PublicAffairs, **2010.**

8. Huber, Peter, *Hard Green,* Basic Books (Perseus Books Group) New York, xv, **1999.**

9. In fact, I am quite the opposite of a "climate change denier." If I may use an old bromide: "Not only do I resent the allegation,

I resent the allegators." I firmly believe that climate is ever-changing. It's happened many times in the geologic past and it is certain to happen again. I have no problem accepting that the Earth may be getting warmer. I simply do not believe that mankind is the primary cause of climate change, nor is 100 years enough time to judge climate trends, considering that the Earth has been around for about 4.5 billion years (that's 4,500,000,000). Requiring Americans to sacrifice their standard of living for something that may not even be happening is folly. Indeed, even if warming is conclusively shown to be occurring, mankind's attempts to stop it will be futile and a monumental waste of money. (See Chapter 6.)

10. Goldberg, Bernard, *100 People Who Are Screwing Up America (and Al Franken is #37)*, HarperCollins Publishers, 85, **2005.**

11. Ibid., p 86

12. Ibid., p 87.

13. Napolitano, Andrew, *Theodore and Woodrow*, Thomas Nelson Inc., 5, **2012**; see also p 45, p 53 and p 194.

14. Zubrin, Robert, *Merchants of Despair*, Enterprise Books, 126, **2012.**

15. Napolitano, Andrew, *Theodore and Woodrow*, Thomas Nelson Inc., 93, **2012**

16. Goldberg, Jonah, *Liberal Fascism*, Doubleday, 255, **2007.**

17. Napolitano, Andrew, *Theodore and Woodrow*, Thomas Nelson Inc., 94, **2012.** Robert Zubrin also wrote extensively about the origins of eugenics (*Merchants of Despair*, Enterprise Books, 35-67, **2012**); Zubrin discussed the role of noted progressive Margaret Sanger, who wanted to use eugenics as a means of population control using sterilizations (ibid., p 88) and abortions (ibid., p 61). He quoted Sanger's mantra as follows: "More children from the fit, less from the unfit" (ibid., p 87).

18. en.wikipedia.org/wiki/Planned_Parenthood

19. Evans, M. Stanton, *Blacklisted by History*, Crown Forum, 601, **1999.**

20. Ibid, 605.
21. Coulter, Ann, *Treason*, Three Rivers Press, 71, **2003.**
22. Ibid, 27.
23. Haynes, John Earl, and Klehr, Harvey, *Venona*, Yale University, **1999.**
24. Romerstein, Herbert, and Breindel, Eric, *The Venona Secrets*, Regnery Publishing, **2000.**
25. Haynes, John Earl and Klehr, Harvey, *In Denial*, Encounter Books, **2003.**
26. ibid. p 9.
27. ibid. p 27.
28. Romerstein, Herbert, and Breindel, Eric, *The Venona Secrets*, xv, Regnery Publishing, **2000.**
29. Haynes, John Earl and Klehr, Harvey, *In Denial*, Encounter Books,8, **2003**
30. Lewis, J, *American Thinker*, "The Evidence for Neocommunism," October 7, 2007. Link to americanthinker.com and search archives for neocommunism.
31. Alinsky, Saul, *Rules for Radicals*, Vintage Books (Division of Random House), 116, **1971.**
32. Ibid, p 33.
33. Zubrin, Robert, *Merchants of Despair*, Enterprise Books, 125, **2012.**
34. Coulter, Ann, *Mugged*, Sentinel (Penguin Group), 178, **2012.**
35. Goldberg, Jonah, *Liberal Fascism*, Doubleday, 53, **2007.**
36. Mark Levin called modern liberals with such beliefs "statists." Levin, Mark R., *Liberty and Tyranny*, Threshold Editions, 4, **2009.**
37. For conservative views, read *Treason* by Ann Coulter, *Liberal Fascism* by Jonah Goldberg and *Liberty and Tyranny* by Mark Levin.
38. Short, Philip, *Pol Pot*, Henry Holt and Co., **2004**; see also Brinkley, Joel, *Cambodia's Curse*, Public Affairs (Member of the Perseus Books Group), **2011.**
39. Short, Philip, *Pol Pot*, Henry Holt and Co., 327, **2004.**

40. Loung Ung, *First, They Killed My Father*, HarperCollins, **2001**.

Chapter 3 The Democrat Party

1. I was apprehensive about discussing Democrat demographics and voting blocs because of the vitriol that leftists pour upon anyone who dares examine the constituencies of the Democrat party. Often, leftists make charges of racism, even though such a charge may be completely groundless. However, in the final analysis, I decided that it would be impossible to discuss decline of America without broaching this topic. Both Ann Coulter in *Mugged* and Bernard Goldberg in *100 People Who Are Screwing Up America* have written about racial demagoguery and braved the inevitable charges of racism and abuse from the left.

2. www.census.2010.gov

3. Fund, John and von Spakovsky, Hans, *Who's Counting?*, Encounter Books, **2012**; see also Brink, Ben, *The Dead Always Vote Democrat*, McAlester Publishing, **2012**.

4. www.jewishvirtuallibrary.org/jsource/Judaism/jewpop.html

5. Thomas, Clarence, *My Grandfather's Son*, HarperCollins, 270, **2007**.

6. ibid. p 257.

7. blogs.orlandosentinel.com/news_politics/2010/10/goerge-will-brands-grayson-americas-worst-politician.html

8. Coulter, Ann, *Mugged*, Penguin Group, 14, **2012**; see also H. Hudson, www.humanevents.com/2011/07/10/democrats-should-know-jim-crow-they-created-him/.

9. Miller, Zell, *A National Party No More*, Stroud & Hall Publishing, 119, **2003**

10. Ibid, p 67; see also p 100.

11. Ibid, p 96.

12. Ibid., p 68.

13. ibid. p 60

14. ibid. p 18; See also Bryce, Robert, *Power Hungry*, PublicAffairs, 291, **2010;** Bryce was arguing against the Iowa caucus having undue influence on the selection of presidents. He felt Iowa, as the biggest corn-producing state, influenced candidates to support the harmful "corn ethanol boondoggle."

Chapter 4 Energy and the Environment

1. Reisch, Marc S., *Chemical & Engineering News*, 12, November 19, 2012.
2. Moore, John A. and Shute, Toby, *The Hidden Cleantech Revolution*, Energy Publishers of America, 94, **2010**.
3. Ibid, p 4.
4. Bryce, Robert, *Gusher of Lies*, PublicAffairs, 224, **2008**; see also p 220.
5. Bryce, Robert, *Power Hungry*, PublicAffairs, 39, **2010;** see also p 96.
6. Lomborg, Bjørn, *The Skeptical Environmentalist*, Cambridge University Press, 129, **2001**.
7. sustainablenuclear.org/PADs/pad0506comby.pdf
8. wikipedihttp://en.wikipedia.org/wiki/
9. Yucca_Mountain_nuclear_waste_repositorya.
10. Moore, John A. and Shute, Toby, *The Hidden Cleantech Revolution*, Energy Publishers of America, 65, **2010**.
11. Ibid. p. 69.
12. "A 'play' is a combination of trap, reservoir rock, and seal that has been shown by previously discovered fields to contain commercial petroleum deposits in an area." N. J. Hyne, *Nontechnical Guide to Petroleum Geology, Exploration, Drilling, and Production*, PennWell Corporation, 207, **2001**.
13. A "waterless" method using liquefied petroleum gas as the fracking fluid has been developed. This is among the new environmentally improved options that can be used. See **gasfrac.com**

14. Zubrin, Robert, *Merchants of Despair*, Encounter Books, 1, **2012**.
15. Ibid, p 2
16. Ibid., p 98.
17. Bryce, Robert, *Gusher of Lies*, PublicAffairs, 145, **2008**; for a discussion of the fallacies of "cellulosic ethanol" see Bryce, Robert, *Power Hungry*, PublicAffairs, 179, 2010.
18. Lomborg, Bjørn, *The Skeptical Environmentalist*, Cambridge University Press, 136, **2001**.

Chapter 5 Foreign Policies and the UN

1. Goldberg, Jonah, *Liberal Fascism*, Doubleday, 11 (**2007**).
2. wikipedia.org/wiki/USS_Cole_bombing
3. Offner, Arnold (editor), *America and the Origins of World War II*, Houghton Mifflin Co., v, **1971**.
4. Napolitano, Andrew, *Theodore and Andrew*, Thomas Nelson, Inc., 103 (**2012**); see also Goldberg, Jonah, *Liberal Fascism*, Doubleday, 158 (**2007**).
5. Prange, Gordon, *At Dawn We Slept*, Penguin Books, 287, **1981**.
6. Ibid., p 169
7. wikipedia.org/wiki/United_States_military_casualties_of_war.
8. Chang, Iris, *The Rape of Nanking*, Penguin Books, 1997.
9. Goldberg, Jonah, *Liberal Fascism*, Doubleday, 122 (**2007**); see also Napolitano, Andrew, *Theodore and Andrew*, Thomas Nelson, Inc., 137 (**2012**).
10. Goldberg, Jonah, *Liberal Fascism*, Doubleday, 122 (**2007**).
11. Though the subject of this chapter is *foreign* policy, I've included a few words about FDR's domestic policies to illustrate the extent of powers he assumed while in office. They also support of my contention that FDR was virtually a dictator in the 1930s, during which he presided over a huge expansion of government. His socialistic "New Deal" brought about transformative changes in the structure of government and established run-

away bureaucracies, some of which bloat government to this day.

12. During the Tet Offensive, which started on January 31, 1968, the US and allies suffered about 4100 killed. However, the communists were estimated to have lost about 58,000. Dunnigan, James and Nofi, Albert, *Dirty Little Secrets of the Vietnam War*, Thomas Dunne Books, 50, **1999**. For a brief discussion of communist atrocities in Hue during Tet, see Karnow, Stanley, *Vietnam—A History*, Penguin Books, 531, **1983**. Tet was a disaster for the communists, but it was portrayed by the mainstream media of the time as an American defeat.

13. historyplace.com/speeches/ford-tulane.htm

14. nation.foxnews.com/us-embassy-attack/2012/09/17/goodwin-mideast-obamas-chickens-are-coming-home-roost.

15. http://en.wikipedia.org/wiki/Mohamed_Morsi

16. http://www.nytimes.com/2013/01/15/world/middleeast/egypts-leader-morsi-made-anti-jewish-slurs.html

17. http://www.un.org/en/documents/charter/chapter1.shtml

18. http://www.discerningtoday.org/members/Digest/2000Digest/December/global_governance_is_here.htm; *see also* http://www.climatedepot.com/a/1893/Gore-US-Climate-Bill-Will-Help-Bring-About-Global-Governance

19. Bate, Roger, Tren, Richard and Roberts, Donald, http://www.aei.org/article/health/global-health/the-united-nations-scientific-fraud-against-ddt.

20. http://www.reuters.com/article/2009/05/06/us-ddt-idUSTRE54542W20090506.

21. Zubrin, Robert, *Merchants of Despair*, Encounter Books, 93, **2012**.

22. http://unfccc.int/essential_background/convention/background/items/1353.php; see also wikipedia.org/wiki/United_Nations_Framework_Convention_on_Climate_Change

23. wikipedia.org/wiki/Intergovernmental_Panel_on_Climate_Change.

24. http://www.thenewamerican.com/world-news/asia/
    item/12049-un-slammed-for-its-forced-abortions-in-china-
    using-us-funds
25. http://www.usnews.com/science/articles/2009/11/18/
    un-fight-climate-change-with-free-condoms).

Chapter 6 The Global Warming Boondoggle

1. John Brignell's list of things caused by global warming (reproduced with permission):

   *Agricultural land increase, Africa devastated, African aid
   threatened, Africa hit hardest, air pressure changes, Alaska
   reshaped, allergies increase, Alps melting, Amazon a desert,
   American dream end, amphibians breeding earlier (or
   not), ancient forests dramatically changed, animals head
   for the hills, Antarctic grass flourishes, anxiety, algal blooms,
   archaeological sites threatened, Arctic bogs melt, Arctic in
   bloom, Arctic lakes disappear, asthma, Atlantic less salty,
   Atlantic more salty, atmospheric defiance, atmospheric
   circulation modified, attack of the killer jellyfish, avalanches
   reduced, avalanches increased, bananas destroyed,
   bananas grow, beetle infestation, bet for $10,000, better
   beer, big melt faster, billion dollar research projects, billions
   of deaths, bird distributions change, bird visitors drop, birds
   return early, blackbirds stop singing, blizzards, blue mussels
   return, bluetongue, boredom, bridge collapse (Minneapolis),
   Britain Siberian, British gardens change, brothels struggle,
   bubonic plague, budget increases, Buddhist temple
   threatened, building collapse, building season extension,
   bushfires, business opportunities, business risks, butterflies
   move north, cancer deaths in England, cardiac arrest,
   caterpillar biomass shift, challenges and opportunities,
   childhood insomnia, Cholera, circumcision in decline, cirrus*

disappearance, civil unrest, cloud increase, cloud stripping, cockroach migration, cod go south, cold climate creatures survive, cold spells (Australia), computer models, conferences, coral bleaching, coral reefs dying, coral reefs grow, coral reefs shrink , cold spells, cost of trillions, cougar attacks, cremation to end, crime increase, crocodile sex, crumbling roads, buildings and sewage systems, cyclones (Australia), damages equivalent to $200 billion, Darfur, Dartford Warbler plague, death rate increase (US), Dengue hemorrhagic fever, dermatitis, desert advance, desert life threatened, desert retreat, destruction of the environment, diarrhoea, disappearance of coastal cities, diseases move north, Dolomites collapse, drought, drowning people, ducks and geese decline, dust bowl in the corn belt, early marriages, early spring, earlier pollen season, Earth biodiversity crisis, Earth dying, Earth even hotter, Earth light dimming, Earth lopsided, Earth melting, Earth morbid fever, Earth on fast track, Earth past point of no return, Earth slowing down, Earth spinning out of control, Earth spins faster, Earth to explode, earth upside down, Earth wobbling, earthquakes, El Niño intensification, erosion, emerging infections, encephalitis, equality threatened, Europe simultaneously baking and freezing, evolution accelerating, expansion of university climate groups, extinctions (human, civilisation, logic, Inuit, smallest butterfly, cod, ladybirds, bats, pandas, pikas, polar bears, pigmy possums, gorillas, koalas, walrus, whales, frogs, toads, turtles, orang-utan, elephants, tigers, plants, salmon, trout, wild flowers, woodlice, penguins, a million species, half of all animal and plant species, not polar bears, barrier reef, leaches), experts muzzled, extreme changes to California, fading fall foliage, famine, farmers go under, fashion disaster, fever,figurehead sacked, fir cone bonanza, fish catches drop, fish catches rise, fish stocks at risk, fish stocks decline, five million *illnesses, flesh eating disease, flood patterns change, floods, floods of beaches and cities, Florida economic decline, food poisoning, food prices rise, food security threat (SA), footpath erosion, forest decline, forest expansion, frostbite, frosts, fungi fruitful, fungi invasion, games change, Garden of Eden wilts, genetic diversity decline, gene pools slashed, gingerbread houses collapse, glacial earthquakes, glacial retreat, glacial growth, glacier wrapped, global cooling, global dimming, glowing clouds, god melts, golf Masters wrecked, Gore omnipresence, grandstanding, grasslands wetter, Great Barrier Reef 95% dead, Great Lakes drop, greening of the North, Grey whales lose weight, Gulf Stream failure, habitat loss, Hantavirus pulmonary syndrome, harvest increase, harvest shrinkage, hay fever epidemic, hazardous waste sites breached, health of children harmed, heart disease, heart attacks and strokes (Australia), heat waves, hibernation ends too soon, hibernation ends too late, homeless 50 million, hornets, high court debates, human development faces unprecedented reversal, human fertility reduced, human health improvement, human health risk, hurricanes, hurricane reduction, hydropower problems, hyperthermia deaths, ice sheet growth, ice sheet shrinkage, illness and death, inclement weather, infrastructure failure (Canada), Inuit displacement, Inuit poisoned, Inuit suing, industry threatened, infectious diseases, inflation in China, insurance premium rises, invasion of cats, invasion of herons, invasion of midges, island disappears, islands sinking, itchier poison ivy, jellyfish explosion, Kew Gardens taxed, kitten boom, krill decline, lake and stream productivity decline, lake shrinking and growing, landslides, landslides of ice at 140 mph, lawsuits increase, lawsuit successful, lawyers' income increased (surprise surprise!), lightning related insurance claims, little response in the atmosphere, lush growth in rain forests,*

Lyme disease, Malaria, malnutrition, mammoth dung melt, Maple syrup shortage, marine diseases, marine food chain decimated, marine dead zone, Meaching (end of the world), megacryometeors, Melanoma, methane emissions from plants, methane burps, melting permafrost, Middle Kingdom convulses, migration, migration difficult (birds), microbes to decompose soil carbon more rapidly, monkeys on the move, Mont Blanc grows, monuments imperiled, more bad air days, more research needed, mountain (Everest) shrinking, mountains break up, mountains taller, mortality lower, mudslides, National security implications, new islands, next ice age, Nile delta damaged, no effect in India, Northwest Passage opened, nuclear plants bloom, oaks move north, ocean acidification, ocean waves speed up, opera house to be destroyed, outdoor hockey threatened, oyster diseases, ozone loss, ozone repair slowed, ozone rise, Pacific dead zone, personal carbon rationing, pest outbreaks, pests increase, phenology shifts, plankton blooms, plankton destabilised, plankton loss, plant viruses, plants march north, polar bears aggressive, polar bears cannibalistic, polar bears drowning, polar bears starve, polar tours scrapped, porpoise astray, profits collapse, psychosocial disturbances, puffin decline, railroad tracks deformed, rainfall increase, rainfall reduction, rape wave, refugees, reindeer larger, release of ancient frozen viruses, resorts disappear, rice threatened, rice yields crash, riches, rift on Capitol Hill, rioting and nuclear war, rivers dry up, river flow impacted, rivers raised, roads wear out, rockfalls, rocky peaks crack apart, roof of the world a desert, Ross river disease, ruins ruined, salinity reduction, salinity increase, Salmonella, salmon stronger, satellites accelerate, school closures, sea level rise, sea level rise faster, seals mating more, sewer bills rise, sex change, sharks booming, sharks moving north, sheep shrink, shop closures, shrinking *ponds, shrinking shrine, ski resorts threatened, slow death, smaller brains, smog, snowfall increase, snowfall heavy, snowfall reduction, societal collapse, songbirds change eating habits, sour grapes, space problem, spiders invade Scotland, squid population explosion, squirrels reproduce earlier, spectacular orchids, stormwater drains stressed, street crime to increase, suicide, taxes, tectonic plate movement, teenage drinking, terrorism, threat to peace, ticks move northward (Sweden), tides rise, tourism increase, trade barriers, trade winds weakened, tree beetle attacks, tree foliage increase (UK), tree growth slowed, trees could return to Antarctic, trees in trouble, trees less colourful, trees more colourful, trees lush, tropics expansion, tropopause raised, tsunamis, turtles crash, turtles lay earlier, UK Katrina, Vampire moths, Venice flooded, volcanic eruptions, walrus displaced, walrus pups orphaned, war, wars over water, wars threaten billions, water bills double, water supply unreliability, water scarcity (20% of increase), water stress, weather out of its mind, weather patterns awry, weeds, Western aid cancelled out, West Nile fever, whales move north, wheat yields crushed in Australia, white Christmas dream ends, wildfires, wind shift, wind reduced, wine - harm to Australian industry, wine industry damage (California), wine industry disaster (US), wine - more English, wine -German boon, wine - no more French , winters in Britain colder, wolves eat more moose, wolves eat less, workers laid off, World bankruptcy, World in crisis, World in flames, Yellow fever.*

2. D. B. Malpass, *Introduction to Industrial Polyethylene*, Scrivener and John Wiley & Sons, 100 (**2010**); C. Goodyear, *San Francisco Chronicle*, March 28, 2007.

3. For example, see *Earth 2100*, produced in 2009 by ABC. It depicts the life of the fictional character "Lucy" and how global warming affected her.

4. D. Horowitz, *The Professors*, Regnery Publishing, Inc., 139, **2006**.

5. Simmons, John G., *The Scientific 100, Fall River Press*, 299, **2009**; published originally by Kensington Publishing Corp. in 1996.

6. en.wikipedia.org/wiki/List_of_**New_York_hurricanes**

7. en.wikipedia.org/wiki/**Intergovernmental_Panel_on_Climate_Change**

8. Booker, Christopher, The Real Global Warming Disaster, Continuum Publishing, 48 (**2009**).

9. ipcc.ch/working_groups/working_groups:

    Working Groups 2 and 3 are concerned how governments should respond to climate change IPCC Working Group II (WG II) assesses the vulnerability of socio-economic and natural systems to climate change, negative and positive consequences of climate change, and options for adapting to it. It also takes into consideration the interrelationship between vulnerability, adaptation and sustainable development. The assessed information is considered by sectors (water resources; ecosystems; food & forests; coastal systems; industry; human health) and regions (Africa; Asia; Australia & New Zealand; Europe; Latin America; North America; Polar Regions; Small Islands).

    The IPCC Working Group III (WG III) assesses options for mitigating climate change through limiting or preventing greenhouse gas emissions and enhancing activities that remove them from the atmosphere. The main economic sectors are taken into account, both in a near-term and in a long-term perspective. The sectors include energy, transport, buildings, industry, agriculture, forestry, waste management. The WG analyses [sic] the costs and

benefits of the different approaches to mitigation, consid-
ering also the available instruments and policy measures.
The approach is more and more solution-oriented.

10. Spencer, Roy, *The Great Global Warming Blunder*, Encounter Books, xv, **2010**.

11. en.wikipedia.org/wiki/List_of_scientists_opposing_the_mainstream_scientific_assessment_of_global_warming.

12. Hayden's letter to Lisa Jackson, then EPA Administrator, is reproduced (with permission) below:

I write in regard to the Proposed Endangerment and Cause or Contribute Findings for Greenhouse Gases Under Section 202(a) of the Clean Air Act, Proposed Rule, 74 Fed. Reg. 18,886 (Apr. 24, 2009), the so-called "Endangerment Finding."

It has been often said that the "science is settled" on the issue of CO_2 and climate. Let me put this claim to rest with a simple one-letter proof that it is false.

The letter is s, the one that changes model into models. If the science were settled, there would be precisely one model, and it would be in agreement with measurements.

Alternatively, one may ask which one of the twenty-some models settled the science so that all the rest could be discarded along with the research funds that have kept those models alive.

We can take this further. Not a single climate model predicted the current cooling phase. If the science were settled, the model (singular) would have predicted it.

Let me next address the horror story that we are approaching (or have passed) a "tipping point." Anybody who has worked with amplifiers knows about tipping points. The output "goes to the rail." Not only that, but it stays there. That's the official worry coming from the likes of James Hansen (of NASAÂGISS) and Al Gore.

But therein lies the proof that we are nowhere near a tipping point. The earth, it seems, has seen times when the CO_2 concentration was up to 8,000 ppm, and that did not lead to a tipping point. If it did, we would not be here talking about it. In fact, seen on the long scale, the CO_2 concentration in the present cycle of glacials (ca. 200 ppm) and interglacials (ca. 300-400 ppm) is lower than it has been for the last 300 million years.

Global-warming alarmists tell us that the rising CO_2 concentration is (A) anthropogenic and (B) leading to global warming.

(A) CO_2 concentration has risen and fallen in the past with no help from mankind. The present rise began in the 1700s, long before humans could have made a meaningful contribution. Alarmists have failed to ask, let alone answer, what the CO_2 level would be today if we had never burned any fuels. They simply assume that it would be the "pre-industrial" value.

 ► The solubility of CO_2 in water decreases as water warms, and increases as water cools. The warming of the earth since the Little Ice Age has thus caused the oceans to emit CO_2 into the atmosphere.

(B) The first principle of causality is that the cause has to come before the effect. The --historical record shows that climate changes precede CO_2 changes. How, then, can one conclude that CO_2 is responsible for the current warming?

Nobody doubts that CO_2 has some greenhouse effect, and nobody doubts that CO_2 concentration is increasing. But what would we have to fear if CO_2 and temperature actually increased?

- A warmer world is a better world. Look at weather-related death rates in winter and in summer, and the case is overwhelming that warmer is better.
- The higher the CO_2 levels, the more vibrant is the biosphere, as numerous experiments in greenhouses have shown. But a quick trip to the museum can make that case in spades. Those huge dinosaurs could not exist anywhere on the earth today because the land is not productive enough. CO_2 is plant food, pure and simple.
- CO_2 is not pollution by any reasonable definition.
- A warmer world begets more precipitation.
- All computer models predict a smaller temperature gradient between the poles and the equator. Necessarily, this would mean fewer and less violent storms.
- The melting point of ice is 0 °C in Antarctica, just as it is everywhere else. The highest recorded temperature at the South Pole is -14 °C, and the lowest is -117 °C. How, pray, will a putative few degrees of warming melt all the ice and inundate Florida, as is claimed by the warming alarmists?

Consider the change in vocabulary that has occurred. The term global warming has given way to the term climate change, because the former is not supported by the data. The latter term, climate change, admits of all kinds of illogical attributions. If it warms up, that's climate change. If it cools down, ditto. Any change whatsoever can be said by alarmists to be proof of climate change.

In a way, we have been here before. Lord Kelvin "proved" that the earth could not possibly be as old as the geologists said. He "proved" it using the conservation of energy. What he didn't know was that nuclear energy, not gravitation, provides the internal heat of the sun and the earth.

Similarly, the global-warming alarmists have "proved" that CO_2 causes global warming.

Except when it doesn't.

To put it fairly but bluntly, the global-warming alarmists have relied on a pathetic version of science in which computer models take precedence over data, and numerical averages of computer outputs are believed to be able to predict the future climate. It would be a travesty if the EPA were to countenance such nonsense.

13. Michael Crichton in Author's Message in *State of Fear;* HarperCollins Publishers, 571, **2004**:
14. Howard Hayden, *A Primer on CO_2 and Climate*, Vales Lake Publishing, 24, **2008**.
15. S. Fred Singer, *Hot Talk Cold Science*, The Independent Institute, 5, **1998**; see also Robert Carter, *Climate: The Counter Consensus*, Stacey International, 75 **2010**. An excellent discussion of glaciation cycles and the variability of climate is available in a book by G. Dendrick Robinson and Gene D. Robinson, *Global Warming: Alarmists, Skeptics & Deniers*, Moonshine Cove Publishing, **2012**.

16. en.wikipedia.org/wiki/Water_vapor#Water_vapor_in_ Earth.27s_atmosphere. The concentration of water in the atmosphere varies greatly and is highly dependent upon temperature. Water vapor may be present in the atmosphere up to about 4% (40,000 ppm) in the tropics, but can also be as low as a few hundred ppm in a very cold climate, *e.g.*, Antarctica.

17. Howard Hayden, *A Primer on CO2 and Climate*, Vales Lake Publishing, 25, **2008**.

18. en.wikipedia.org/wiki/Ozone_depletion .

19. D. B. Malpass, *Introduction to Industrial Polyethylene*, Scrivener Publishing and John Wiley & Sons, 23, **2010**.

20. P. Huber, *Hard Green*, Basic Books (Perseus Books Group) New York, xiv, **1999**.

21. Howard Hayden, *A Primer on CO2 and Climate*, Vales Lake Publishing, 33, **2008**.

22. ibid., 37.

23. Michael Crichton, *State of Fear*, HarperCollins Publishers, 570, **2004**.

24. Deidre Lockwood, *Chemical & Engineering News*, 26, December 17, 2012.

25. Robert Carter, *Climate: The Counter Consensus*, Stacey International, 212, **2010**; see also J. Adler, *Global Warming and Other Eco-myths*, Competitive Enterprise Institute, (R. Bailey editor), 279, **2002**. *"Vorsorgeprinzip"* is discussed by Robert Zubrin, (*Merchants of Despair*, Encounter Books, 203, **2012**).

26. Michael Crichton "was an American best-selling author, producer, director, and screenwriter, best known for his work in the science fiction, medical fiction, and thriller genres" (http://en.wikipedia. org/wiki/Michael_Crichton). Several of his views on global warming and the environment were listed in his Author's Message in his novel *State of Fear* (HarperCollins Publishers, 571, **2004**):

- ► *We know astonishingly little about every aspect of the environment from its past history [sic], to its present state, to how to conserve and protect it...*
- ► *We are also in the midst of a natural warming trend that began about 1850, as we emerged from a four-hundred-year cold spell known as the "Little Ice Age."*
- ► *Nobody knows how much of the present warming trend might be a natural phenomenon.*
- ► *Nobody knows how much of the present warming trend might be man-made.*
- ► *Before making expensive policy decisions on the basis of climate models, I think it is reasonable to require that those models predict future temperatures accurately for a period of ten years...*
- ► *There are many reasons to shift away from fossil fuels, and we will do so in the next century without legislation, financial incentives, carbon-conservation programs, or the interminable yammering of fearmongers. So far as I know, nobody had to ban horse transport in the early twentieth century.*
- ► *We desperately need a nonpartisan, blinded funding mechanism to conduct research to determine appropriate policy. Scientists are only too aware whom they are working for. Those who fund research—whether a drug company, a government agency or an environmental organization— always have a particular outcome in mind. Research funding is almost never open-ended or open-minded. Scientists know that continued funding depends on delivering results the funders desire. As a result, environmental organization "studies" are every bit as biased and suspect as industry "studies." Government "studies" are similarly biased according to who is running the department or administration at the time. No faction should be given a free pass.*

27. Robert Carter, *Climate: The Counter Consensus*, Stacey International, 212, **2010**.

28. J. Adler, *Global Warming and Other Eco-myths*, Competitive Enterprise Institute, (R. Bailey editor), 265, **2002**.

29. From the *Bulletin of Atomic Scientists (www.thebulletin.org › Media Center › Announcements)*:

> *Human activities are now the dominant cause of global climate change. Emissions of heat-trapping gases continued to climb in 2012, with atmospheric levels of carbon dioxide -- the most important greenhouse gas affected by human activities -- reaching levels higher than at any time in the past 800,000 years. 2012 was the hottest year on record for the contiguous United States. Arctic sea ice continued to rapidly diminish in extent, reaching a record low this past year that fell under the previous low by an area the size of Texas. Glaciers are retreating, and the massive Greenland and Antarctic ice sheets are losing mass. Extreme weather events, such as last year's Superstorm Sandy and Typhoon Bopha, now strike in an environment altered by climate change, with higher sea surface temperatures and more water vapor in the atmosphere to fuel and sustain their destructive power.*

Yet another hyperbolic statement that begins with a falsehood and continues with misleading pronouncements without perspective intended to scare the public.

30. Various authors, *Chemical and Engineering News*, 12, 16, 22, February 18, 2013.

31. Robert Carter, *Climate: The Counter Consensus*, Stacey International, 5, **2010**.

Additional suggested reading on the anthropogenic global warming hoax:

- C. C. Horner, *Red Hot Lies*, Regnery, **2008**.

- G. Dendrick Robinson and Gene D. Robinson, *Global Warming: Alarmists, Skeptics & Deniers*, Moonshine Cove Publishing, **2012**.

- Patrick Michaels, *Meltdown*, Cato Institute, **2004**.

- Henrik Svensmark and Nigel Calder, *The Chilling Stars—A New Theory of Climate Change*, Icon Books, **2007**.

- Robert Higgs and Carl Close (editors), *Re-thinking Green— Alternatives to Environmental Bureaucracy*, The Independent Institute, **2005**.

- Patrick Michaels and Robert Bolling, Jr., *Climate of Extremes*, Cato Institute, **2009**.

- Patrick Michaels (editor), *Shattered Consensus*, Rowman & Littlefield, **2005**.

- S. Fred Singer and Dennis Avery, *Unstoppable Global Warming*, Rowman & Littlefield, **2007**.

- Roy Spencer, *Climate Confusion*, Encounter Books, **2008**.

- Patrick Michaels and Robert Bolling, Jr., *The Satanic Gases*, Cato Institute, **2000**.

- DL Ray and L Guzzo, *Environmental Overkill*, HarperCollins, **1993**.

- C.C Horner, *The Politically Incorrect Guide to Global Warming and Environmentalism*, Regnery, **2007**.

- I. Murray, *The Really Inconvenient Truths*, Regnery, **2008**.

Chapter 7 Taxes and Voting

1. York, Byron, *Washington Examiner*, August 6, 2012, http://washingtonexaminer.com/york-when-1099-felons-vote-in-race-won-by-312-ballots/article/2504163. See also Fund, John and von Spakovsky, Hans, *Who's Counting?*, Encounter Books, 13, **2012**

2. http://www.nbcnews.com/id/51148666/ns/local_news-wichita_falls_tx/t/cincinnati-poll-worker-faces-charges-voting-times-november/. For more detailed discussions of voting improprieties, see Brink, Ben, *The Dead Always Vote Democrat*, McAlester Publishing, **2012** and Fund, John and von Spakovsky, Hans, *Who's Counting?*, Encounter Books, **2012**.

3. Brink, Ben, *The Dead Always Vote Democrat*, McAlester Publishing, 40, **2012**. See also Fund, John and von Spakovsky, Hans, *Who's Counting?*, Encounter Books, **2012** and http://www.americanthinker.com/2012/11/voter_fraud_redefined.html, by Matthew Vadum, November 8, 2012.

4. In a *CNN* column, liberal LZ Granderson asked, *should ignorant people be allowed to vote?* He goes on to say: *If we weed out the ignorant voters, politicians will no longer feel the need to dumb down the conversation in hopes of getting their attention.* Further, Granderson wrote: *Weed out some of the ignorant by making people who want to vote first pass a test modeled on the one given to those who want to become citizens.* Granderson, LZ, cnn.com/2011/09/27/opinion/granderson-broken-government-voters.

The San Francisco Examiner reported that former congressman and presidential candidate Tom Tancredo said in a keynote address he delivered to the first National Tea Party Convention in 2010: *We do not have a civics literacy test before people can vote. People who could not even spell the word 'vote' or say it in English put a committed socialist ideologue in the White House.*

Conservative commentator and political writer Jane Chastain applauded Tancredo's comments and went one step further. In a commentary found on *WorldNet Daily*. Chastain wrote: *In this country, voting is a lot like Russian roulette or shooting darts, blindfolded.* Referring to the motor-voter bill, Chastain said: *Liberals will not be happy until everyone who can fog a mirror is registered to vote.*

5. Hagler, Frank, http://www.policymic.com/articles/15182/voter-suppression-laws-political-iq-tests-would-ensure-citizens-are-qualified-to-vote
6. R Hernstein and C. Murray, *The Bell Curve*, Free Press Paperbacks (Division of Simon & Schuster), 128, **1995**; see also wikipedia.org/wiki/War_on_Poverty;).
7. Robert Rector, nationalreview.com/articles/229326/losing-war/robert-rector

Chapter 8 Political Correctness and Higher Education

1. Orwell, George, *1984*, originally published in 1949 by Martin Secker & Warburg, Ltd. Also published by Heritage Publishers (India) in 2005 and many others. Search Amazon.com for George Orwell to see other publishers.
2. S. D. Alinsky, *Rules for Radicals*, Vintage Books (Division of Random House), 3, **1971**.
3. D. Horowitz, *The Professors*, Regnery Publishing, Inc., p xxxiii, **2006**.
4. ibid., p xlvi.
5. D. Horowitz, *The Professors*, Regnery Publishing, Inc., **2006**. The list of Horowitz's "most dangerous academics in America" is as follows:

Professor	School
M. Shahid Alam	Northeastern University
Hamid Algar	University of California, Berkeley
Lisa Anderson	Columbia University
Gil Anidjar	Columbia University
Anatole Anton	San Francisco State University
Bettina Aptheker	University of California, Santa Cruz
Sami al-Arian	University of South Florida
Leighton Armitage	Foothill College
Stanley Aronowitz	City University of New York
Regina Austin	University of Pennsylvania
Bill Ayers	University of Illinois, Chicago
Ihsan Bagby	University of Kentucky
Amiri Baraka	Rutgers University, Stony Brook
David Barash	University of Washington
Hatem Bazian	University of California, Berkeley
Marc Becker	Truman State University
Joel Beinin	Stanford University
Derrick Bell	New York University
Marvin Berlowitz	University of Cincinnati
Mary Frances Berry	University of Pennsylvania
Michael Berube	Penn State University
Laurie Brand	University of Southern California
Elizabeth Brumfiel	Northwestern University
Thomas Castellano	Rochester Institute of Technology
Noam Chomsky	Massachusetts Institute of Technology
Kathleen Cleaver	Emory University
Dana Cloud	University of Texas, Austin
David Cole	Georgetown University
Juan Cole	University of Michigan
Miriam Cook	Duke University
Patrick Coy	Kent State University

Hamid Dabashi	Columbia University
Angela Davis	University of California, Santa Cruz
Gregory Dawes	North Carolina State University
Nicholas De Genova	Columbia University
Bernadine Dohrn	Northwestern University
Robert Dunkley	University of Northern Colorado
Michael Eric Dyson	University of Pennsylvania
Rick Eckstein	Villanova University
Paul Ehrlich	Stanford University
Marc Ellis	Baylor University
Mark Ensalaco	University of Dayton
John Esposito	Georgetown University
Larry Estrada	Western Washington University
Matthew Evangelista	Cornell University
Richard Falk	Princeton University
Sasan Fayazmanesh	California State University, Fresno
Joe Feagin	Texas A&M University
Gordon Fellman	Brandeis University
Norman Finkelstein	De Paul University
Eric Foner	Columbia University
John Bellamy Foster	University of Oregon, Eugene
H. Bruce Franklin	Rutgers University
Grover Furr	Montclair State University
Melissa Gilbert	Temple University
Todd Gitlin	Columbia University
Lewis Gordon	Temple University
Jose Angel Gutierrez	University of Texas, Arlington
Yvonne Haddad	Georgetown University
Warren Haffar	Arcadia University
Tom Hayden	Occidental College
Caroline Higgins	Earlham College
James Holstun	State University of New York, Buffalo

bell hooks	City University of New York
Alison Jaggar	University of Colorado, Boulder
Frederic Jameson	Duke University
Leonard Jeffries	City University of New York
Robert Jensen	University of Texas, Austin
Ron (Maulana) Karenga	California State University, Long Beach
Peter Kirstein	Xavier University (Chicago)
Vinay Lal	University of California, Los Angeles
Jerry Lembcke	Holy Cross College
Mark LeVine	University of California, Irvine
Robert McChesney	University of Illinois, Champaign-Urbana
Aminah Beverly McCloud	De Paul University
Manning Marable	Columbia University
Joseph Massad	Columbia University
Mari Matsuda	Georgetown University
Ali al-Mazrui	State University of New York, Binghamton
Oneida Meranto	Metropolitan State College, Denver
Armando Navarro	University of California, Riverside
Victor Navasky	Columbia University
Priya Parmar	Brooklyn College
Emma Perez	University of Colorado, Boulder
Sam Richards	Penn State University
Gayle Rubin	University of Michigan, Ann Arbor
Dean Saitta	University of Denver
Orville Schell	University of California, Berkeley
Michael Schwartz	State University of New York, Stony Brook
Eve Kosofsky Sedgwick	City University of New York

Timothy Shortell	Brooklyn College
Harry Targ	Purdue University
Greg Thomas	Syracuse University
Suzanne Toton	Villanova University
Haunani-Kay Trask	University of Hawaii, Manoa
Michael Vicino	University of Rhode Island
Michael Warner	Rutgers University
Dessima Williams	Brandeis University
George Wolfe	Ball State University
Howard Zinn	Boston University

6. ibid., p xxvi.
7. ibid., p xlvi.
8. For example, referring to Arabs or other people from the Middle East as "ragheads." Many Americans are clueless about the difference between a Sikh wearing a turban and a Saudi wearing a traditional keffiyeh. That may be more a consequence of ignorance rather than bigotry. Nonetheless, neither Sikhs nor Saudis should be subjected to such denigrating names. There are numerous other examples of spiteful name-calling having to do with ethnicity and race which will not be discussed here. I agree completely that such names are offensive and should not be used as a simple matter of civility and decorum. Thankfully, those who use such names are few in number.
9. Carol Platt Liebau, townhall.com/columnists/carolplattliebau/ 2011/09/05/obama_uses_euphemism_to_obscure_his_ unpopular_agenda/page/full/
10. http://www.strategicvision.com/press_release.php?pr=42
11. I recognize that there are consumers who buy hybrids and electric cars because they want to save money by dramatically reducing use of expensive gasoline. However, I believe few have done a thorough cost-benefit analysis to see if the added cost is worth the savings in gas. Even with subsidies, the cost of the hybrid or all electric car will be significantly more than a similarly

equipped ICE car. Liberals will probably not care and will view this as the cost of being politically correct.

As indicated in Chapter 4, hybrids are growing in popularity and are certain to remain an important segment in the automotive industry. Though presently expensive, hybrids are reliable, practical alternatives to vehicles powered by ICE. Not so for the all electric car. Unless the drawbacks mentioned in Chapter 4 are resolved, electric cars will remain a minor part of the automotive market. Indeed, they might disappear altogether because of poor sales, not to return until the technology becomes more practical and affordable to the average citizen. See the analysis of hybrids and the all electric car by Robert Bryce (*Power Hungry*, PublicAffairs, 187, **2010**).

If President Obama is able to destroy the American oil industry, as it appears he wants to do, the payout on hybrids may become more attractive. If so, Mr. Obama will have succeeded in getting the cost of gasoline up, perhaps to $6-8 per gallon. Concomitantly, he will have irreparably damaged the US economy and raised the cost-of-living for Americans to unacceptable heights.

12. Coulter, Ann, *Demonic*, Crown Forum, 119, **2011**.
13. http://nacc.stanford.edu/mascot.html
14. http://en.wikipedia.org/wiki/University_of_California,_Santa_Cruz#Mascot
15. http://keepingscore.blogs.time.com/2009/05/17/top-10-worst-college-team-names/slide/the-university-of-hawaii-rainbow-warriors
16. http://en.wikipedia.org/wiki/Washington_Wizards

Chapter 9 Corruption and Incompetence in Government

1. Corruption in President Obama's administration was discussed at length by Michelle Malkin (*Culture of Corruption*, Regnery Publishing, **2009**.) She was writing about Obama administration abuses after only 6 months in office. Imagine the additional abuses since mid-2009 perpetrated by the Obama administration!

2. Kurtzleben, D, http://www.usnews.com/news/articles/2012/11/19/how-the-nations-interest-spending-stacks-up

3. Miller, Dennis, *The O'Reilly Factor*, Fox News Channel, February 13, 2013, billoreilly.com/show?action=viewTVShow&showID=3 327D Miller.

4. This is a famous quote from Mel Brooks portraying King Louis 14th of France in his 1981 satiric movie *History of the World, Part 1*.

5. http://blog.heritage.org/2012/12/26/morning-bell-obamas-ap-and-trade-scheme-for-cars/

6. Lomborg, Bjørn, *The Skeptical Environmentalist*, Cambridge University Press, 207, **2001**.

7. Anderson, Jeffrey, http://blog.heritage.org/2011/04/06/new-analysis-reveals-obamacare-will-cost-more-than-expected/

8. http://en.wikipedia.org/wiki/List_of_federal_judges_appointed_by_Jimmy_Carter.

9. http://en.wikipedia.org/wiki/California_Proposition_187_(1994))

10. McDonnell, Patrick, *Los Angeles Times*, November 15, 1997. http://articles.latimes.com/1997/nov/15/news/mn-54053).

11. http://www.legalzoom.com/lawsuits-settlements/personal-injury/top-ten-frivolous-lawsuits

12. http://www.washingtontimes.com/blog/inside-politics/2012/may/16/obama-budget-defeated-99-0-senate/

13. http://www.gallup.com/poll/161210/congress-approval-stagnant-low-level.aspx

14. http://www.discoverthenetworks.org/individualProfile.asp?indid=981. The complete quote is as follows: *During a 2005 visit to the Jet Propulsion Laboratory in California, Lee asked a guide whether the Mars Pathfinder had taken a photograph of the flag planted on Mars by Neil Armstrong in 1969.* (Armstrong's 1969 mission, of course, was to the Moon, not Mars.)

15. Goldberg, Bernard, *100 People Who Are Screwing Up America*, Harper Collins, 58, **2005**.

Chapter 10 Where Do We Go from Here?

1. Wade, Lisa, thesocietypages.org/socimages/2012/11/14/u-s-racialethnic-demographics-1960-today-and-2050/, November 14, 2012.

2. Passel, Jeffery and Cohn, D'Vera, pewsocialtrends.org/files/2010/10/85.pdf, February 8, 2008.

3. http://www.usnews.com/news/articles/2012/11/19/how-the-nations-interest-spending-stacks-up

4. Granderson, LZ, cnn.com/2011/09/27/opinion/granderson-broken-government-voters.

5. Methanol doesn't exhibit many of the drawbacks of other alternative fuels such as hydrogen, which is a gas that is difficult to handle and forms highly explosive mixtures with air. Like gasoline, methanol is a liquid at normal handling temperatures. It is inexpensive, abundantly available, and may be derived from either fossil fuels or biomass. Unlike ethanol, methanol doesn't require fermentation and may be produced from biomass other than food crops. However, the raw material that will be the most economical for the production of methanol for the foreseeable future will be natural gas (methane). Even in the case of methanol, extensive revisions to the "fuel infrastructure"

(flex-fuel engines, storage tanks, pumps, etc.) will be required, but that is true of any foreseeable alternative. See Olah, G. A., Goeppert, A. and Prakash, G. K. Surya, *Beyond Oil and Gas—The Methanol Economy*, Wiley-VCH, **2006**. See also Zubrin, Robert, *Merchants of Despair*, Enterprise Books, 242, **2012**.

6. http://en.wikipedia.org/wiki/Secession_in_the_United_States
7. http://en.wikipedia.org/wiki/
   Cascadia_(independence_movement)
8. http://news.yahoo.com/blogs/news/
   northern-colorado-wants-secede-colorado-174432609.html
9. Naylor, Thomas, *Secession: How Vermont and All the Other States Can Save Themselves from the Empire*, Feral House, **2008**.
10. Excerpted from DL Ray and L Guzzo, *Environmental Overkill*, HarperCollins, 207, **1993**.

Epilogue

1. http://en.wikipedia.org/wiki/
   Fourteenth_Amendment_to_the_United_States_Constitution
2. http://www.npr.org/templates/story/
   story.php?storyId=129201845.
3. Steyn, Mark, *America Alone*, Regnery Publishing, 56, **2006**.

APPENDIX A

(Answers to questions in Chapter 7)

▶ What are the three branches of the US government?

    d) Legislative, executive and judicial

▶ How many senators are elected from each state?

    a) 2

▶ Which political party favors strong defense, lower taxes, and limited government?

    a) Republican

▶ How many states currently make up the USA?

    c) 50

▶ In what years did the US fight in The Second World War?

    b) 1941-1945

▶ What do North Korea, Cuba and China have in common?

    a) They are all communist states

▶ Who became president when Franklin Roosevelt died in 1945?

    d) Harry Truman

▶ How many justices sit on the Supreme Court?

    c) 9

▶ Which president was responsible for *The Great Society* program?

    b) Lyndon Johnson

- ▸ Which president was responsible for *The New Deal*?

    b) Franklin Roosevelt

- ▸ How many Representatives are elected from each state?

    d) Depends on population of state

- ▸ Which president was responsible for establishing the EPA and OSHA?

    d) Richard Nixon

- ▸ Which of the following were among the Axis countries opposing the US in World War II?

    d) Italy, Japan and Germany

INDEX

ABOUT THE AUTHOR

Dennis B. Malpass was born and raised in Biloxi, Mississippi. He attended Tulane University in New Orleans, LA and received a BS in chemistry in 1966. He then attended graduate school at the University of Tennessee in Knoxville, TN and studied Main Group organometallic chemistry under Professor Jerome F. Eastham. He received his PhD in organic chemistry in 1970 and began his industrial career with Texas Alkyls, Inc. (now AkzoNobel) in La Porte, TX.

His industrial career spanned 33 years working primarily on synthesis, characterization and applications of metal alkyls. He retired in 2003 and now lives in Magnolia, TX and consults in the petrochemical industry. He has more than 80 patents and publications. He served as sole author of an introductory text on polyethylene, published in 2010. He also served as co-author (with Elliot I. Band) of an introductory text on polypropylene, published in 2012. Both books were published jointly by Scrivener Publishing and John Wiley & Sons. He has taught college and continuing education courses in organic chemistry and polyolefin catalysts. Please send comments and suggestions on the book to:

kaw62jry@gmail.com

www.ingramcontent.com/pod-product-compliance
Lightning Source LLC
Chambersburg PA
CBHW070637290526
45790CB00001B/123